*How to Teach School
and Make a Living at the Same Time*

How to Teach School and Make a Living at the Same Time

PATRICK H. CROWE

SHEED ANDREWS AND McMEEL, INC.
SUBSIDIARY OF UNIVERSAL PRESS SYNDICATE
KANSAS CITY

Library of Congress Cataloging in Publication Data
Crowe, Patrick H
  How to teach School and make a living at the same time

  1. Teachers—Supplementary employment.   I Title
LC2843.S9C76   331.7'61'3711   78-24164
ISBN 0-8362-2605-4
ISBN 0-8362-2600-3 pbk

This Book is Dedicated to:

1. MARC MURDOCK:

Twenty-eight years ago my algebra teacher,, for fifteen years a fellow math teacher, a great help to me, a friend, the most brilliant man I know. I wish we were still teaching together—you'll read more about him.

2. ED SMITH:

Of the folks I know I admire Ed most. You'll read about Ed, too.

3. ME:

'Cause I wrote it and I'm proud of it. (Now THAT'S vanity.)

Contents

Acknowledgments

My thanks to a student of mine (name unfortunately forgotten) who asked in class one day after I had reviewed a book (title unfortunately forgotten), "Why don't you write a book?" I replied, not at all seriously, "The only thing I know enough to write about is how to make a living and teach at the same time."

Thanks also to a member of our English department, Mike Kelly, who, having been told of my comment by one of our students who thought I was serious, said, "I'll buy a copy of your book as soon as it's finished." Mike's copy will be free. Their collective encouragement got me started.

Special thanks to Tom Drape, associate editor at Sheed Andrews and McMeel. His individual encouragement kept me going, and his help was priceless in getting finished. And lest his little brother, Joe (who suggested I contact SA&McM), feel slighted, special thanks to Joe Drape, too.

Introduction

My twofold purpose for writing this book is: (1) to make money; and (2) to share with other teachers a significant part of my educational philosophy, namely, TO BE A FULL-TIME TEACHER AND MAKE A LIVING AT THE SAME TIME.

I believe that many once-dedicated teachers are no longer teaching because they felt the need for more money to support their families. I know some teachers who, along with their families, have sacrificed many material things to stay in teaching.

In one sense, I admire their dedication, yet I do not believe such sacrifices are necessary.

I faced the same dilemma: successful teacher who loved teaching but with a teaching income sure to impose strain and sacrifice on a growing family. Years ago, I wrote, "We want teachers dedicated to teaching, not to poverty." I've now spent nearly twenty years in the classroom and may remain for twenty more. I feel my dilemma has been resolved, the sacrifices minimized, and this book will hopefully tell teachers how to do the same.

This book is not a get-rich-quick scheme. There are only two ways I know to do that: inherit money or marry someone who has it. If you spent your money hoping this book would tell you how to get rich quick, you're going to be disappointed. It won't. I hope it will tell you how to make a decent living while still teaching full time.

I'll close my introduction with a comment that's probably already obvious to the teachers of English composition. I come to this work not as a trained writer. To me, the hallmarks of good writing are clarity and brevity. I'll try for the former and promise the latter. If you expected more pages or better style for your money, I'm sorry. My feeling is that the shorter and more concise I can make this, the more apt you are to read it and that's what I'm hoping you'll do—so here it is.

December 1977

Teachers' Pay

Profession? Professional Pay?

Most of you already know it's a strain to raise a family on a teacher's salary. Whatever your teaching salary is, I hope to show you how to add 50 to 100 percent to it. That is my *hope*—to tell you how to do so—to encourage you TO STAY IN TEACHING AND MAKE A LIVING AT THE SAME TIME.

Now for the *fact*. I have done it and will tell you how.

So far you agree. What you make as a teacher is little more than half what you need. You feel you are not paid as a professional should be. Well, you're not. Now, is that to say you are not a professional? Frankly, I have some reservations about whether teaching in America is a profession.

To me, a profession has the following characteristics:
1. A profession must have the welfare of society as a basic concern.
2. A profession must have an essential body of knowledge that can be passed on to new members.
3. A profession needs to have a unique function.

4. Professions are essentially intellectual; they may include skills, but these are secondary.
5. Professions are autonomous.
6. Professions practice strict control of entry.
7. Professions control the behavior of their members, usually through a strictly enforced code of ethics.

When I ask myself if teaching has these characteristics—or to what extent it has them—the answer is anything but adequate. I wouldn't argue the list is perfect; you may be able to think of some crazy occupation that has all the characteristics and is obviously not a profession. If you can, that's Okay. It's not easy to draw a simple list, so draw your own if mine's faulty. In any case, as I perceive teaching, it passes on numbers one through four—I say passes: it doesn't get As and maybe not Bs, but I'd pass it. I admit that the "unique function" could start a lot of arguments. I'm aware that educators see the function somewhat differently or at least with varying degrees of emphasis. By stating the function with sufficient vagueness, I believe the controversy will be minimized. I'll call it "learning."

I'm also a little worried about the combined implication of numbers two and four: "an essential body of knowledge" to pass on and "essentially intellectual." If a profession is essentially intellectual and also is to have a body of knowledge, there is an implication to be drawn about the intelligence of the members. I know I.Q. tests may be a narrow way to judge intelligence, but for whatever it's worth, there are two studies on educators that are very revealing. According to one study, the Army used a test for possible deferment that showed 68 percent of people in science had I.Q.s over 120 and that of people in education, only 27 percent had correspondingly high I.Q.s. In Florida, a study of 250 elementary school principals revealed an average I.Q. of 104.

Now I know that these are the sort of statistics that one can do more tricks with than a monkey with a mile-and-a-half of grapevine. Still, my experience tends to confirm that our ranks are not filled with high I.Q.s. I'd bet the average among doctors is well above that of teachers. Even so, I'll give teaching a passing mark, maybe only a C-. I know it can be argued that high I.Q.s might be bad for teachers, but I doubt it. I'll take high ones to low ones every time if all other factors are the same. But enough about these first four characteristics. It's the last three that cause the real trouble.

The autonomy may squeak by. Some teachers see themselves as having it and some don't. I'd give it a D- at best, but the next two are Fs.

Control of Entry or What One Must Do to Become a Teacher

True, one has to be licensed to teach. States require that. In most cases, you are required to have completed the right courses and received a degree and then you can get a license. I'm licensed for *life* in Missouri. Get that, for LIFE. I never took an exam to demonstrate to the state examiners that I know my subject. All I did was submit transcripts. The examiners counted course hours and mailed me my license. I'm sure glad they don't do that for doctors. Though it is by no means an absolute guarantee, I find it somewhat reassuring to know that my doctors have passed state board exams. I know that doesn't make them good doctors, but at least they had to know some medicine when they took the exams. I teach math and I've met some teachers, especially in elementary grades, whose knowledge of math was deficient and dislike for math obvious and intense. How these people teach arithmetic is questionable. I suspect they pass along their dislike to the kids, and so we find many students turned off math and ignorant of it.

Still, today, there's very little control of entry. Some states require exams and, granted, being able to pass an exam in one's subject area would not guarantee that one would be a good teacher. Clearly there is no such guarantee. Yet a demonstrable knowledge of one's field is an absolute prerequisite to teaching it. I believe a state board exam to be a more reliable means of judging than counting hours on a transcript. So I give the "profession" low marks on control of entry.

As for a strictly enforced code of ethics, the National Education Association has a code of ethics. Yet how are they to enforce it? What is the possible sanction? Are they going to monitor my teaching and, if they discover I can't solve a simple equation, refuse me membership? If there is anything like a strongly enforced code of ethics in this "profession," I fail to observe it. I doubt if there's even a strong desire to police the ranks. I perceive the National Education Association and the American Federation of Teachers as competing for members, not trying to ensure quality teaching or eliminate inferior teachers. I am not opposed to these organizations. I favor what they're doing. But neither these organizations nor any others that I know of do much to guarantee that teaching will meet my description of the professional.

If you perceive teaching in America as a profession, that's fine with me. I have known or taught with many truly professional teachers, and I'm confident you probably have too. So be it. We may disagree on whether teaching is a profession but I suspect we certainly agree it doesn't pay like other professions, such as medicine or law. So why teach?

Why Teach? Why Not?

You know the reasons you teach. Like any job, there are advantages and disadvantages. I see the advantages as:

- Service to one's fellowman.
- Seeing and experiencing the joy of learning.

- Appreciation from the students.
- Shorter hours than some jobs.
- Longer and more frequent vacations than most jobs.

I conclude my list by adding that teaching is fun. I believe most people know this fun. There seems to be a little teacher in all of us. Whether it's teaching your son to ride his bike or showing a neighbor how to tune that lawnmower that's always been hard to start, it's fun. I'll leave it to the psychologists to tell us why, but to me, seeing someone learn is a real pleasure, no matter the circumstances. Let me add that I know many businessmen who teach part-time—almost with more pride and passion than they do their usual work and usually for far less pay, sometimes free. It seems to me that they really welcome the chance to teach. I suspect they would do more of it if they could. They know the FUN. They are flattered to be asked to share their knowledge and experience. They may even envy the teachers the fun they have teaching full time, and at the same time, they're thinking, "It pays so poorly." So, it is a joy to teach and it is unpleasant to be poorly compensated.

But now to the list of disadvantages. There's one big disadvantage: relatively low pay. Depending on where you teach and how many years you've been at it, I feel safe in saying that your salary is over $8,000 and under $22,000. A few beginners may make less and a few old-timers may make more, but most elementary and secondary teachers in America are in that range. And I'd venture a guess that 90 percent of us are in the $10,000- to $18,000-a-year bracket.

Pay in Private Schools

I believe my remarks thus far about teachers' pay are true for almost all elementary and secondary schools in America. Urban or rural, public or private, the pay is low. My experience tells me it's usually very, very low in private schools.

The school I teach at now is private. That's sort of the code word used when we don't want to give you too much information about it all at once. Actually, it's a Catholic school. Now, I'm not about to build a case for private being better than public or public better than private. That's a can of worms. I believe there are many more similarities than there are differences between private and public schools. I do not teach "Catholic" math. The days of adding six rosaries to four rosaries are long gone, and I'm glad of it. I'd teach math the same way in a public school and I have. So, while I feel there are more similarities than differences, there are two significant differences: (1) Parochial schools usually pay even less than public ones; and (2) in parochial schools, we teach religion or theology.

I think the two differences when combined lead to a strange and ironic conclusion. Within the theology taught in Catholic schools, we find the encyclicals of the various popes, and among those encyclicals, one finds a good bit about such things as the rights of the worker, the living wage, the responsibilities of a just employer.

Here's the irony of it all. I know many teachers in these schools. I have relatives teaching in them and I have taught in four Catholic high schools in three states. On the average, they are paid far less than public schoolteachers; I'd guess 15 to 20 percent less. The school I teach at now pays about the same as the public schools, but the vast majority pay far less. Now, isn't it ironic that these very institutions that are teaching about workers' rights, living wages, and employers' responsibilities to employees are paying even less than the public schools?

You know what the administrators of these institutions are apt to say when asked about this situation. They've all said it to me: "We'd like to pay you more, but we just don't have the money, just can't afford it." That, I suspect, is the same answer given by the employers who used to run the dawn-to-dusk sweat shops. Here's my answer to them, and it's almost twenty-five years old. I'm afraid it's just as true today as when it was written by Brother Joseph Panzer, S.M.

"The Catholic education system is founded on sacrifice. The great majority of our lay teachers fully appreciate this fact and realize if they are to become an integral part of such a system, they must evince a generous measure of devotedness that cannot be evaluated or rewarded in terms of financial remuneration. In the past, many of our lay teachers have cheerfully served for woefully inadequate salaries, feeling as one of their members expressed it, that 'shining like stars for all eternity is not poor recompense for instructing others onto justice.'

"This is a noble sentiment, which we rightfully admire and applaud, but few if any of us are so unrealistic as to think that our lay teachers can long subsist in this world on the promise of such reward, spiritually consoling though it might be. All of them must eat, and dress, and live in proper circumstances; many of them must support young and growing families; all of them, for their own self-respect and the respectability of our educational system, must strive to improve themselves professionally. And all of this unquestionably takes money.

"The problem of adequate salaries for lay teachers is sometimes thought to be a thorny one. But much of its complexity vanishes when we accept the irrefutable premise that if we hire lay teachers at all, we must, in simple justice, pay them a living wage. No amount of argumentation, based as it sometimes is on the meagerness of our financial resources or the multiplicity of our needs, can obscure this elemental moral obligation, or ease our consciences when we have failed to meet it."

Amen, Brother! Amen!

If you teach in one of these schools, then at salary

time next year, pass the above quote around. When you do, be sure to underline the last two sentences in red for the copy that goes to the administration. I'll give the Catholic school administrators the same message in four words: practice what you preach.

So teachers' pay is generally low and, in private schools, usually lower still.

Coping

Teachers have dealt with this low-pay situation in many ways. It would appear that the pay can't be too discouraging—many more teachers are available than teaching jobs and still more graduate each year. I guess many others besides myself find that the advantages outweigh the disadvantages. As I said, it's fun.

In an effort to find out how others cope with the situation, I surveyed our married male faculty. The results were that about 85 percent of our married men had either a working wife, one or more part-time jobs, or other sources of income (only me).

In the questionnaire, I restricted part-time jobs to those not school-related; i.e., directors of extra-curricular activities were not to count those as part-time jobs. Summer jobs were not included either. We had fry cooks, hardware store clerks, probation officers, night school teachers. The list was long, and one man had three part-time jobs.

The working wife was quite common, also. Usually it was more a necessity than a desire to work. I realize it's difficult to determine if a wife works just out of necessity or out of desire. In many cases, it's a combination of both. Still, the common reply seemed to be, "We need the money."

The survey showed very few who supported their families only by teaching. One man, with either six or seven children at the time, was able to and I had to have more details. He admitted it was a real struggle but they got by. He did tell me two things that I shall not soon forget. The first was that almost all of their clothing came from garage sales or used clothing stores. Okay, I accept that one. The second was that his house cost less than my wife's new car. Now, she's not driving a Rolls or even a Mercedes. It's a *Ford*—a house that cost less than a Ford—OUCH! That seemed to illustrate for me how real the disadvantages can be.

I hope it also serves notice to those considering teaching as a career that it can be a life of financial sacrifice, part-time jobs, or working wives. If you're considering teaching, don't expect to raise a family on your teaching pay. A recent government survey of families in this area showed that a family of four needed an income of about $17,200. Believe me, that's not going to leave you wondering what to do with the leftover money. Sure, it's above the poverty level but I suspect that you, as an educated person, may well have developed tastes which would be very difficult to satisfy with that level of income. It seems ironic to be an educated person—perhaps one who can appreciate symphonies, the arts, one who would choose the best schools for his children, one whose value system understands the need for giving to charities—only to find that on a teacher's income, you just don't have the money for such things.

A few words about working wives—it's neither good nor bad. My wife worked before the children were born and, briefly, part-time after. We saved most of her earnings and she never planned to work full time and try to raise a family, too. Of course, I know it can be done and is done well in many cases. I'll say more about saving "her" money later. Two points though: the first one to all "nonworking" wives. Calm yourselves, ladies—I know you *do* work, too. I'm using work in the gainful-employment-outside-the-house sense of the word, and I understand that what goes on for a "domestic engineer" is work.

The second point is the serious one. It's nice to have a choice. For those wives who choose to raise families and "work" besides, that's their choice. I'm not sure teachers' wives have a real choice, and that can be troublesome. If your wife has to work so you can teach, that takes away the choice. To me, that's a disadvantage and a serious one. To be able to teach only by getting one's wife to help support the family can be a high price to pay. It could be hard on the male ego. Clearly, having the choice is nicer.

If teaching and raising a family demand real financial sacrifice and strain, or demand ongoing part-time jobs, or demand a working wife or combinations of these, then I say it's time to look for other ways to teach and make a living.

So—how about raising your teaching pay?

Improving the Present

Three things to do to raise your teaching pay:
1. Get a master's degree (preferably in an academic field—they're a bit more marketable). Most systems pay more for a teacher with an M.A. and you will probably need it to stay in education. It may make you a better teacher. Mine has been a help to me. So here's how to get one and minimize the cost:
   ● Go at night as opposed to taking summers or even a full year off.
   ● Apply for scholarships or employer payment plans.
   ● Get grants from the National Science Foundation, the National Institute of Health, GI Bill, etc. (In one year on an NSF grant, I made more money than teaching, had full tuition, books, and travel paid. In the same year, my wife had an NIH grant that paid almost as much as she had been making teaching nursing. We obtained about sixty hours of graduate credit,

one master's degree, and it didn't cost us a cent.

2. Take on extra duty at school. Some systems pay well for extra duty, but most don't. If yours does, do it; if not, don't.

3. Take advantage of merit pay. In one system in which I taught, a group of us designed and got implemented (that was the tricky part) a merit pay plan. It increased some teachers' pay substantially. I'm aware of the lack of popularity for this sort of thing, and the plan we designed is no longer in use. It meant that the administration had to make decisions, and they seemed strained by that. It meant that teachers had to be evaluated, and some of them felt threatened by that. After about five years, the plan died, but in the meantime teachers who were found deserving of merit moved up the salary scale many times faster than they otherwise would have.

I know that the above three ways aren't much help. But please notice that nowhere in the list have I suggested a move to administration. I hope it is conspicuous by its absence. That's not teaching, and I'm opposed to it because it takes you out of the classroom. This section is short, and the suggestions are not much help because the real answer to what can be done to help raise your teaching pay is: very, very little.

A Glimpse at the Future

Will teaching pay get better?
- Enrollment is declining.
- Taxpayers are in revolt.
- There are too many teachers.
- The public is less than pleased with the quality of education.
- Some students feel they have been cheated by the schools (functional illiterates, etc.).

And then . . . there's inflation.

The answer is painfully obvious. Strikes have been common in recent years. Some have been long and bitter, and yet very little real gain has come to the teachers in terms of purchasing power. I hope to see the day when the major focus of strikes is to improve the quality of education; i.e., smaller classes, better facilities, and so on. That's not to imply that once the quality of education is improved, the teachers will finally get much better pay. I do not believe that will happen. It would be a very long and slow process if it did. It would arrive a bit late for this generation of teachers.

The future of American education looks a bit grim. The chances of significant pay increases appear very remote. If you're waiting for that to happen, I hope you are very patient. I see very little chance that it will, and I'll not be shocked if the situation worsens.

In fact, I have seen serious deterioration in salaries in

just the last three years. It is actually worse than many realize. What follows is a case study of salaries which I recently did for our school. Its purpose was to compare salary increases to increases in the cost of living. The salary figures used are mine—the only ones I knew for sure.

A CASE STUDY OF XYZ HIGH SCHOOL TEACHERS' SALARIES AND THE INCREASED COST OF LIVING FROM 1974 TO 1977

I. *The Increased Cost of Living*

According to the Labor Department's Bureau of Labor Statistics, the percent increase in the Consumer Price Index for the years in question is:

Year	Percent Increase
1974	11.0
1975	9.1
1976	5.8
1977	6.5

These percentages represent the necessary increase in salary in order to maintain the same purchasing power as in the previous year.

II. *The XYZ High School Salaries*

For the purpose of this study, I have chosen a salary

near the top of the master's scale. The choice was dictated by the fact that the data were available in terms of actual salary paid during the period in question.

Year	Salary
1974(5)*	$14,040
1975(6)	15,445
1976(7)	16,225
1977(8)	16,685

* *academic year beginning in 1974*

III. The Comparison

If the 1974 salary of $14,040 had been increased by 11 percent (the CPI for that year), then an equal amount of purchasing power would have been maintained for 1975 (i.e., no raise in real dollars).

If this equivalent salary in 1975 had then been increased by 9.1 percent (the CPI for 1975), then an equal amount of purchasing power would have been maintained for 1976.

If this equivalent salary in 1976 had then been increased by 5.8 percent (the CPI for 1976), then an equal amount of purchasing power would have been maintained for the following year.

If this salary is now increased by 6.5 percent (the CPI for 1977), then the result shows what salary is necessary now to have the same purchasing power as the original $14,040 had in 1974.

The arithmetic of this calculation shows that the necessary salary now to have the same purchasing power as $14,040, is $19,157.

Comparing this "cost of living adjusted" figure to the actual figure, $16,685, it is clear that the actual figure would have to be increased by $2,472 in order to have maintained the same purchasing power as in 1974.

IV. *Conclusions*

1. It appears from Table II that there have been some substantial increases in salary for the years considered in this case study.

2. As substantial as these increases appear to be and as costly as they have been to the employer, they are far short of sufficient to maintain 1974 purchasing levels.

3. If raise is taken to mean the increase in real purchasing power, then there have been no raises.

4. If raise means increase in purchasing power, not only have the salaries not been raised but they have fallen and are now over $2,400 less than is needed to maintain purchasing power.

5. The trend of these data seems to show a steady decline when measured in purchasing power.

6. In one view, the salary in this case has been increased by $2,645 (from $14,040 to $16,685) in a four-year period, but in terms of purchasing power, it would have to be currently increased by another $2,472 to equal its 1974 purchasing power.

Your situation may not be this grim. It's easy to find out by using your own salary figures and making the same calculations. Incidentally, once you've done the arithmetic, feel free to use all or any part of this case study in an effort to help your salary situation. Give it to other teachers, administrators, board members, parents. It's not a magic formula, but still I feel it focuses in a concrete and digestible way on the situation and how it's been deteriorating. Watch out, though—it may make you mad.

I gave this case study to selected teachers and had copies for anyone who wanted them. The original went to the man most directly influencing salaries.

In its original form the case study was five pages long and could have been done in two or three. That's by design, not accident. I'm a strong believer in sending the message to folks in its most readable form and, to me, that calls for few words per page (reader then feels he's reading fast, making progress, will keep going), minimum number of thoughts per page organized as logically as possible, especially if containing numbers.

I can't report any great results from it. The teachers liked it, but the reply I got from our president indicated we were not committed to keeping pace with inflation (ouch!) and he would understand if I had to seek employment elsewhere because of loss of real purchasing power (ouch! grrrr! ugghh! and phooey!). Still, I feel it made the point, and I suspect it had some small influence toward raising salaries a bit. A few weeks after the report, my contract was offered to me—a 4.3 percent increase—further deterioration. But then, without my case study, it might have been less and it took only one afternoon to write it.

I'll conclude my glimpse at the future with what must be all too painful: you're not apt to get more money (real raises) by teaching. So, if you don't want to have a part-time job all your life and you don't want to put pressure on your wife's choice about working, then how do you make a living as a teacher? Read on!

2

The Money Mentality

Here's what you need to make money:
- Willingness to take risks.
- Willingness to work.
- Perseverance.
- Passion.

Life's Risky—So Are Christmas Trees

My first venture was the Christmas tree business at the retail level. I hardly knew a pine tree from a fir tree. I had a friend who was willing to spend some time during the day, and I was willing to work after school and on weekends. He had no capital, and I had only modest savings (from my wife's working) that were planned for use as a down payment on a house. It took most of my savings to buy the trees, rent the lot, get lights, etc. I remember the what-ifs: What if I lose our savings? What if the trees burn? What if they are stolen? What if no one will buy them? What if we don't get good trees? As I look back now, it seems to me that on any venture I've ever tried or even considered, there have always been a number of people kind enough to tell me all the reasons not to try it. They mean well, but they are negative thinkers. One very easy thing to do is find reasons not to do something. I suspect that these negative thinkers will be saying in their old age, "Well, maybe if I'd tried that when I was younger, I'd have more today." In fact, they have said that all along; they were always too old or too young or too something. They plod along taking as few chances as possible. Avoid these people or you'll never take any risks and will wind up missing all the excitement.

In that first venture, we paid as little as a dollar each for some trees and as much as a dollar a foot for others. It all ended with not enough profit to pay the lost interest on my savings. I think we netted four cents an hour for our efforts and were left with hundreds of trees to dispose of. My friend and I can sit now and laugh about it. What part of our fannies we didn't work off we froze off, but I wouldn't trade 1 percent of that memory and experience for 100 percent of all the negative "what-if" sort of advice I've gotten in twenty years.

It taught us we could work together, that hard work and determination could make up for a lot of ignorance. Today, twenty years later, we're still partners in some pretty successful businesses. Most of all, we did then what we have done repeatedly since: took the risk, paid our money, took our chance, and did what we could to make it work.

There were two more years in the Christmas tree business. One was a roaring success. It's unheard of in that business to sell every tree you buy. When the lot gets down to the last two or three dozen trees, it looks so barren that few people will stop. Those who stop find that the trees are picked over. In our second year, we sold every tree and were home counting our money several days before Christmas.

The key to the success was the fact that I'm a teacher. I believe most folks have fond memories of some teacher they had at one time or of some school and that proved critical to our success.

We were searching for a lot from which to sell trees. One hundred dollars was our maximum rent and hopefully less. We passed an empty grocery store of one of the largest national chains. That would be ideal— inside, well lighted, etc. But we knew that no national chain would consider renting for thirty days a building they were trying to lease on a long-term basis. And when they found out it would be filled with trees (fire hazard) and that the total rent would be $100, there was just no way they would do it.

We went to see the real estate manager for the national chain. I'd venture a guess he'd never had a more ridiculous proposal before and probably none since. The risks to him were enormous and the possible gain ($100) couldn't mean much to a national corporation. He listened, he frowned and I'll bet he thought to himself, "I've heard everything now."

"Is this your first year in the tree business?" he asked. "No, it's our second," I said. (No amateurs here, we had experience.) "What else do you do?" he inquired. (I was sure he was just being polite before he would laugh us out of his office.) "I teach school at Podunk," I said. (Now he would know for sure to stay away from us. If this guy was sharp, he certainly wouldn't be teaching school, or so I thought he would be thinking.) "Oh, my son went to school there, loved it. He's married now and made me a grandfather. You know, I don't see why we couldn't do this." (Huh? I thought.) "You guys be careful and clean the place up when you're finished." "Thank you." Fast exit (don't give him time to reconsider), and we sold every last tree.

The third year was no great success: better than the first and not as good as the second. We were early lining up the lot and had quite an unusual corner. In fact, if you've been to Kansas City, you may have seen the Board of Trade building. People know of it because it's there that much of the Midwest's commodities are bought and sold and because it's on the edge of the famous Country Club Plaza. I smile each time I go by it because its construction was delayed a few weeks so I could sell Christmas trees there.

As I said, we lined up the lot early. I'm not sure why the best known real estate firm in the city, the one that developed the Country Club Plaza, agreed in late summer to let us sell trees on that corner. I suspect it was to help out a teacher. In any case, they agreed, only to call in late November to say we couldn't use the lot because they were about to start construction of the Board of Trade building. They offered us alternate locations. Though I had nothing in writing from them, I said, "Sorry, a deal is a deal." There was a long pause and a quick "I'll get back to you." I followed the call with a letter essentially saying fair is fair and pleading for justice. By the time we moved our trees in, the construction equipment was on the scene but they stayed out of our way and we stayed out of theirs.

I learned there are some folks who have a keen sense of keeping their word when they could easily get away with breaking it. It is a good feeling that returns each time I pass the building, and I tell myself it just may have been because the gentleman's keen sense of justice was surrounded by fond memories of one of his teachers.

Take the risk, ignore the "what-ifs," make it work, and it probably won't hurt to let folks know you're a teacher. It's scary, but it's challenging. It's work, but it's fun.

The psychology of making money as well as the basic principles of a free-enterprise system demand that you must be willing to take risks. Small risks followed by success is the stuff such willingness is built on. It's always scary and some folks will always be there telling you not to, but TAKE RISKS. LIFE IS RISKY, SO BE ALIVE

The Swimmer Who's Angry

When it comes to willingness to work, there's one basic motivator for this: need for money. As a teacher, you should have plenty of first-hand experience with that. If you intend to stay in teaching, then it's poverty city or willingness to work. Choose early.

You may have said many times (at least to yourself) that you are willing to work, but that hasn't produced any money. I suspect fear is the cause of your hesitation. When I experience that fear, I choose to recall that I know that out there among all those successful businessmen (making so much money), I'll find a great many who would be scared just to enter a classroom full of thirty-five rambunctious, tough-looking teenagers. Tell these successful businessmen that besides entering the room, they are to bring the group to order, maintain that order, get the kids interested in intellectual things, and then see to it that these thirty-five actually learn (geometry or whatever). Then you'll find out that some of these successful businessmen scare rather easily by teachers' standards. They'd be scared as hell, and you and I have been doing that same thing day in and day out and it doesn't scare us. So don't let fear of the business world limit your willingness to work. Come on in, the water's fine. You can swim as well as the rest of the folks.

There's another way to develop willingness to work. It involves anger and bitterness. I've seen a good many teachers who are angry and even bitter about being so poorly paid. It's very easy to get angry about. Each time you read an article telling of wages for plumbers, you may feel the anger tugging at you. Of course, it's not limited to plumbers. Try garbage collectors. Just a few months ago, the media reported on some garbage collectors who were making $17,500 a year. After teaching ten years and with a master's degree, most teachers don't make that. Can't you hear yourself saying, "At least I should make as much as a garbage man—no, I should make twice as much." Well, you know you don't, and here comes the anger. It gets worse when you have to pay a doctor twenty dollars for a five-minute office visit. You know he's had a lot of training but so have you. Why should he be making more in a month than you do in six months?

So the anger is plentiful, the reminders of your relatively low pay are all too frequent and this sort of repeated anger can easily turn to bitterness. It can produce teachers who are mad at society for mistreating them and for depriving them and their families of the niceties and even some of the necessities of life.

Anger is not a good frame of mind for teachers to be in. Even if it's just sort of a self-pitying "poor teacher" attitude, I don't like it. Enthusiastic teaching takes a lot of energy, and anger and self-pity drain energy. Any teacher knows kids can do plenty to irritate and annoy their teachers, and if you're already half-mad when you enter the classroom, those irritations and annoyances can quickly escalate to anger or even near rage. Such reaction is out of proportion and, of course, the suffering student has no way of knowing the real cause.

There are many ways to deal with anger, and with my fine Irish temper, I've had lots of chances to experiment with the various ways. I've tried reading books on it, going to training sessions about it, and I'll summarize a few ways for you: pillow punching, pencil breaking, crying, hammering, screaming at a mirror, blaming others, running, daydreaming—the list goes on and on.

I was once very angry because I perceived myself as having been treated unjustly by the police. I was attending a training session and described my anger to the trainer. He gave me a doll and told me to take all my anger out on the doll, do whatever I felt like, rip it up, if necessary. I did. It was not much help. In fact, none of the ways I've listed have ever been much help to me. The one thing that helps me is to actually do something about the actual cause of the anger. I guess I can't transfer it. If those work for you, fine. But if you're angry about low pay, I'll tell you what cured my anger—MONEY.

When I experienced that sort of anger, I'd channel it into willingness to work. Long before it grew to bitterness, I'd vent the frustration and anger in hard work.

It can be very productive, superproductive. And it's

a cycle, self-curing. If you're angry about not having enough money, then go to work. The work will diffuse the anger, indefinitely postpone the bitterness, and the income that results will tend to make you forget that you're underpaid as a teacher. It's hard to be mad about not having enough money when you have plenty. Besides, dealing with anger in any constructive way is much more healthy than letting it inevitably turn to bitterness.

Fighting City Hall and Perseverance

A person can develop a lot of perseverance through dealing with the government. It may also be the best testing ground for whatever perseverance you have. The bureaucracy and buckpassing of government have become well known, and these can produce high frustration levels. I developed a dogged sense of perseverance out of frustration and inspiration. The frustration came from the bureaucrats, and the inspiration came from the man I was working with.

Years ago, I was teaching swimming to a group of girls from an inner-city center. Each Saturday morning, I'd load them in my station wagon and head for the YWCA. I was one of three volunteers, and the center was actually a run-down house that had cost $800. One evening, I was asked to come to a meeting about the center and, three hours later, somehow, the center had been completely turned over to the three of us. Then, because of being known in the neighborhood, I was asked to serve on the Model Cities corporate board of directors for the area and, before I knew it, I was the (volunteer) principal executive officer of the corporation.

Model Cities was a Great Society Program to demonstrate that poverty neighborhoods could be made into model neighborhoods. It used federal money administered by the city. Thus, I began dealing with the bureaucracy.

It was wild. The city had about $8 million a year and there were ninety-eight agencies or corporations trying to operate on the money. The task of the corporate officers was to obtain as much of the $8 million as they could for their group. Our share was about $11,000. We were the smallest neighborhood with the lowest census but perhaps some of the greatest needs. We struggled along, and our share of the money gradually increased. The people were very supportive and the corporation decided to hire a neighborhood resident to tend to its affairs—salary: $323 a month. That is how I met Ed Smith. Some houses got repaired, some streets got paved, some curbing was installed, a few new sidewalks. Each project took quite a fight with city hall, but the needs were large and Ed was a persistent fighter.

Model Cities was funded as a five-year program. It was the third year and we had a staff of two, a larger budget, a rented office in the neighborhood, though by no means was it becoming anything like what a model neighborhood should be.

As the end drew near, the question became how to continue the services for the people. Ed Smith, now our director, wanted to propose that Model Cities money be used to build a community center in the neighborhood. That would give us a place for the people that would remain when the program ended. Logic was against a community center: too few people; too late in the program. We asked for it anyway. No chance; all the Model Cities money was under contract and the whole program was soon to phase out. Besides, we had no architectural plans, no ground, and no way to operate it if we did get it built. Asked again and again: no way. There was token sympathy for the cause from the bureaucracy: "You people just don't understand. It may be a nice idea, but it just can't be done."

Ask again. If there was money, could we have a community center? Answer: the money is all spoken for, it is under contract and the programs are closing down. For the final two years, Ed asked, he begged, he argued. The buck got passed and passed and passed. Ed talked to anyone and everyone at city hall, from the mayor to the clerks. They knew what he was after and that he was crazy to think he'd ever get it.

At a public meeting at city hall, we asked. The mayor said it was a good idea but there was no money. Politics! Crowe to mayor: "If there was money, would

you support our proposed center for funding?" Mayor
to Crowe: "There is no money left in the program."
Crowe to mayor: "If, I say if, there was money, would
you support it?" Mayor to Crowe: "Yes." Crowe to
mayor: "May we have a motion to that effect?" Moved,
seconded and passed.

Along came what the bureaucrats call a supplemental grant—an extension—more money. It was too
late for the programs that had already closed and too
small to maintain all the remaining ones. We had not
closed and were now determined to get our center
from the supplemental grant. Ed reminded everyone
he saw in his almost daily trips to city hall that the
mayor had passed a motion supporting our center if
money was available, and now some was.

At the next public meeting, we heard what the
money was going to be used for and it surely wasn't our
center. We reminded everyone at the meeting of the
motion, but the chosen use did have more logic to it.
Still, I saw some real discomfort; not everyone can
break a commitment without feeling it. I angrily raised
the issue and quoted the motion. They did other things
with the money. There was the frustration of dealing
with bureaucrats and, believe me, I was frustrated.

The program ended and, sure enough, what the
bureaucrats call "fall-out funds" began to appear.
Some agencies had not spent all their budgets. Their
staffs had seen the end coming and gotten jobs
elsewhere as they could. In some cases, a staff member

would leave in the last few months of the program, and his empty job slot would not get filled: too near the end to hire someone new. How much were the funds going to amount to? It was wait and see and line up support while waiting.

With most of the agencies closed or defunct, there was less competition for the money. In addition, there was the old motion about what to do with the money if there was any. The city manager got Ed and I in his office and told us the money would not be used for our center. Regardless of any previous motion, he could not possibly justify a community center for our neighborhood. By now, our corporate funding had stopped. Ed was working without pay, our rented office was closed, and our desks and files were moved to the old $800 house.

I think city hall was convinced they'd seen the last of Smith and Crowe. I'm still not sure how Ed survived those next nine months without pay, but he worked every day and kept going to city hall as often as before and plugging away for the center. It must have softened some hard-hearted bureaucrats. People just don't do that. When your pay stops, you stop. Such selfless service was quite an inspiration to me, and I'd fight alongside Ed whenever I could and always when he asked me to.

The fall-out funds piled up, and it was almost another two years to completion, but today there stands in that neighborhood the Dunbar Community

Center. It's mute testimony to the perseverance of Ed
Smith. When it comes to the service of his fellowman,
he's a man who just will not take "no" for an answer,
and I admire him greatly for it.

Persistence, perseverance, determination: It pays
off, it gets things done. It is so strong a force that people
cannot long ignore it. It will win in the end even on the
bureaucrats, and they're a pretty tough test.

I'm afraid this section on perseverance is already a
bit long but it's because it's so all-fired important.
There is no substitute for dogged determination.

One summer while vacationing with my brother, he
told me of the willingness of the university where he
teaches to accept special students. They're notoriously
strict about who they admit and I was skeptical. I really
wanted to believe him but my "crap detector" told me
it was mostly crap. I knew something about his
institution and most of what I knew reinforced my
skepticism.

While driving home, I thought of a student who'd be
ideal for the program. Neighborhood leader, mother
died when he was seven, had seen his father only once,
had completed two years of junior college in five years.
I had seen him work on community projects with great
success and sacrifice. He once quit a construction job to
take a job at our center that paid $50 a week. I knew his
transcripts would be plenty shaky and yet, all I knew
about him convinced me he had the determination that,
if I could ever get him in, he would graduate or die

trying. By the time I hit my driveway, I was determined Ken was soon to go to a famous university.

I asked Ken and he wanted to go. I called my brother, followed the call with a letter, and told Ken to get ready. It wasn't quite that simple. The university wanted ACT or SAT scores. He hadn't taken either. We arranged for the tests and sent in the results. Still, no quick acceptance and summer was ending. His reading scores looked low, so a friend got him enrolled in a reading development program. His pastor sent a letter of recommendation, as did his physics teacher. Ken traveled to the university for an interview but still there was no favorable response.

By now the fall semester had started. I was griped and I was determined. I was going to get him in if I had to buy the whole damn university to do it! (My second official act after putting him in would have been to kick the director of admissions as far off the campus as I could.) I got two players from the Kansas City Chiefs who were alumni of the institution to meet Ken, visit with him, and write letters about their impressions. I had a hunch I'd sent enough information and recommendations to get him made pope, and yet all I wanted was admission to their special program, supposedly designed to admit people just like Ken. Besides that, I had my brother hand-delivering all these letters so they would be sure to get to the right people. I could not have made up details nearly as convincing as the ones in Ken's case. I thought to myself, "Those

admissions people must think we're the damndest
bunch of liars in the state or else their program is not
what they say it is."

Finally, one of those famous "okay, but" sort of
replies arrived. They would accept Ken for the spring
term, *but* he'd get three semesters credit for the four he
had completed (ouch) and there would only be partial
financial aid (foul, low blow). Where the hell did they
think a youngster from the ghetto was going to get a
thousand dollars a semester? That was ten times what it
had cost him for junior college and it was a struggle.

I was tempted to call the director of admissions and
tell him to stick the whole thing in his ear. I'd go on to
tell him that an original hunch of mine had been correct
and that Ken was going to become the first black
Protestant pope instead. I didn't call. Instead, I called a
friend who was active in the university's local alumni
club. He understood perfectly. He told me later the
club showed a little resistance to the idea of giving a
scholarship of $500 a semester, but he crammed it down
their throats before they really had time to gag. The
facts were just that convincing.

Ken was on his way. A full semester had slipped away
to get done what I felt should have taken a letter and a
phone call. By the end of one year, Ken no longer
needed the help of the alumni club and in five
semesters, he was a cum laude graduate.

Making money takes perseverance, but I assure you
it's easier than fighting City Hall or admissions

directors.

There's an extra benefit that comes from perseverance. It's the happy, warm, excited feeling I get in my tummy and across the back of my neck. Each time I think of the years of determination it took to get our community center or the persistence it took to almost force an unwilling university to accept Ken, I get those same exciting feelings all over again. Hanging in there despite the odds is not only winning but feeling good each time you recall it.

I could say even more about it. Persistence, perseverance, dogged determination. Call it what you like. You've probably heard many such stories and may have a few of your own. For clarity and brevity, McDonald's has said it best. I believe what they say, so here it is—just look what it's done for hamburgers.

Press On
Nothing in the world can take the place of persistence. Talent will not; nothing is more common than unsuccessful men with talent. Genius will not; unrewarded genius is almost a proverb. Education alone will not; the world is full of educated derelicts. Persistence and determination alone are omnipotent.

Passion

Passion means attacking jobs rather than working at them. Enthusiasm and decisiveness are the keys—the

damn-the-torpedoes, full-speed-ahead kind of thinking.
Get it done now.

One winter Saturday morning, I was reading the
business opportunity ads as I often do. There it was, a
new ad. I called; it sounded good. I called my partners
and, before going to bed Sunday night, we'd spent
$40,000, had a new business, and were committed to a
renovation that would take more money and lots of
time.

The deal would close in about two weeks and what a
two weeks it turned out to be. We were fairly sure we'd
made a reasonably good investment. Yes, it would have
been nice to buy cheaper, but the price we paid was
reasonable. I was talking to the owner of a similar
business, only to hear of another such business that was
for sale and at a third of the price we'd just paid. I got the
partners together again and, all of a sudden, we had two
new businesses, both in need of renovation.

You may have guessed it—a third such opportunity
surfaced within a week and so we had three, the third
needing major renovation and expansion, though costing only a fourth of the original one.

Before the second deal closed, we had renovated the
first. It took one hell of an attack. There were some 120-
hour weeks and some sore muscles, but renovate it we
did. By the end of the first renovation, the partners were
beginning to ask for air. My method was simple: set a
feverish pace and they would keep up. Partners are like
that. No one wants to be accused of doing less than his

share, so pick out a big share for yourself, attack enthusiastically, and the enthusiasm will become contagious. They will do their damndest to keep up. I've seen similar renovations drag on for months and months, and ours was done in a matter of weeks.

As the second deal was closing, the third was collapsing. Frankly, it was a relief. Such passionate attacks cannot be sustained indefinitely, and I sensed none of us would be able to maintain the pace through three such projects. The third one seemed to loom over us. Sure, we could probably do the second one but, by then, we'd have had it, and just the knowledge of having a third waiting for us seemed like a terrible weight.

With the third deal still possible but doubtful, we attacked the second. One partner balked—too many other responsibilities, he couldn't help. That left the two remaining partners with an extra share to pick up and prompted us to abandon efforts to salvage the third deal.

It was tough and I guess I can recall being pretty tired at the time. But now that it's done, I'm secure in the knowledge that in less than ninety days, we bought, expanded, and completely renovated two small businesses. I like knowing it was done in record time. Within thirty days of the time each deal closed, each had a new image, new customers, and new income. I'm pleased to report that the profit picture on each looks great. One of the former owners returned a few weeks after he sold and he couldn't believe his eyes. If he saw the profit picture now, I'll bet he couldn't believe that either.

I can now attack projects of the magnitude of these because I'd previously done it to many smaller ones.

I've got a trick or two to set myself up for this. It's a bit like getting psyched up for the big game. I need to have the decks cleared so I won't have to stop once I start. Have all the parts, pieces, tools (whatever you'll need to finish) ready before you start. I even get extra sleep beforehand if it's going to be a long one. I like to work late at night because there are no people, no phone calls, absolutely minimum interruptions. I block out a maximum amount of time when I can just keep at it. Set deadlines, promise deliveries, etc. Choose to place yourself in situations where there will be consequences if you don't get done what you said you'd do. That gets things done.

If it's a really big piece of work, organize it into blocks, schedule it, and attack the blocks one at a time. I was even tempted to buy ads for this book before I had it started. Then I'd do it or lose my advertising money. I needed something to get me to do it; it's been put off too many times. (I didn't buy the ads but still may if I get bogged down.)

Of course, this kind of passion is hand in glove with perseverance, and the two spell success. Decide to take the risk, be willing to work (unafraid or angry), attack with full force, and hang in there until you've whipped it.

3

What You Must Do to Teach and Make a Living

START YOUR OWN BUSINESS

I know that probably raises more questions than it answers. How do I start a business? Where do I get the capital to start one? How can I run a business and teach, too? First, let me tell you why it must be your own business.

Profits, Incentives, and Taxes

Profits are better than salary when considering what must necessarily be a part-time venture. Part-timers are usually paid at a lower rate than full-timers. It will take too many hours working for someone else (even at a good salary) to double your teaching income. You don't have the time to do that and teach, too. I had many part-time jobs in my early years and the hourly pay rate was low, usually even lower than teaching pay. The ownership of your own business, not a part-time job, is the means to double your income. They are okay to acquire start-up capital and a good

41

way to learn about business, but it's much more interesting, satisfying, and profitable to own it yourself. In addition, there's almost no chance a part-time job will ever pay really big money. While it's not likely with a part-time business of your own, it's possible. Few part-time jobs pay twenty dollars an hour. I suspect most don't even pay half that, yet that's what I expect to be (and am) paid for managing my businesses, and that's on top of the 10 to 15 percent return I expect on the capital I have invested. Now, that may not be "physician's wages," but it's pretty good by teachers' standards. The first reason it should be your own business is because you can reasonably expect profits to be higher than the salary you get in a part-time job.

The profit incentive is the basis of American business. You'll work harder and more seriously when the results benefit you directly or cost you directly. That's just common sense, isn't it? Aren't you apt to be more conscientious about your own business than about someone else's? Aren't you more apt to give an extra measure of effort when it's your money that's invested? That's not to imply that all employees neglect their duties because it's not their money that's invested. Not so, but it feels different to be the owner. You'll simply be more concerned about the success than if you're an employee. You'll be more willing to give the extra special effort. Ownership demands it and, at the same time, almost guarantees it. So, the second reason is that you'll have the incentive to work harder at it.

Tax advantages are the third reason. Just the investment tax credits and the other ways you can legally avoid paying income taxes are almost enough reason to start a business of your own. Even if it's a slow year getting started or there's a bad year later on, the losses will mean that you'll get to keep more of your teaching pay and, while losses are always unpleasant, as a salaried teacher you have a good bit of income tax to avoid if you can legally do so.

When you own a business, you can likely have certain relatives on the payroll who can make money without being liable to pay federal income tax. Paying one's children for helping in the business is a legitimate business expense and, if they are students, they can make a little over $2000 a year and not pay any federal income tax. Car expenses can be deducted at seventeen cents a mile for some cars (mine), and if you can operate your car for less than that (I do), you can still deduct the full seventeen cents a mile. The difference is tax-free money.

The difficult part of saying more about specific tax advantages is that the tax laws keep changing. Just be very sure that what you're doing is legal. I hear jail is an unpleasant place to pass away the time and besides, you'd probably miss the students.

Once you're in business, either study the tax laws and loopholes very carefully or have someone who is in that business do it for you. And there's an obvious idea for a business of your own: If you've studied the tax laws carefully, there's good money to be made doing other people's tax returns.

Profits, incentives, and tax advantages: those are the reasons it should be a business of your own. But what form should it take? Of the many ways to own a business, I prefer partnerships. A partner can provide the flexibility that your teaching schedule won't allow. He can carry on when you are vacationing or ill. A partnership is inexpensive to form and easy to dissolve. They do have disadvantages, as well. Choose partners with care because either partner can obligate the partnership for debts. (There's more about choosing partners in Chapter 6.) The other choice is to own the whole thing yourself. That, too, has pluses and minuses. I am currently involved in four partnerships or joint ventures and own one small company by myself.

What Business Should A Teacher Own

To me, the five points of focus in choosing what business a teacher should own are: (1) control, (2) hours, (3) employees, (4) return on your money, and (5) cash flow vs. equity accrual.

Who's in Charge Here?

I'll illustrate guideline (1) with my worst financial disaster.

On the staff of one of the schools where I taught was

a brilliant mathematician, Marc Murdock. He had inherited a small fortune, maybe $175,000, and for quite a few years had occasionally bought and sold a few stocks at no great profit or loss. In addition, Marc had made some other moderately profitable investments. His interest in the stock market began to grow. He studied, read the financial magazines and papers, and took a very serious approach. He painstakingly charted (in the very technical sense) many stocks. I watched as he attacked the market with real passion, and I recall that in one year, Marc said he made about $8,500 in the market, almost as much as he was making teaching. The next year, it was attack with full passion and full resources.

Marc was willing to share his information. I've always been a bit skeptical of free advice on the stock market, but I knew how strongly he believed in his data because I knew how heavily he was investing. He was buying a certain stock a thousand shares at a time, and he was borrowing money to do it. I decided to follow along. Each time Murdock bought a thousand shares, Crowe would buy one hundred. I did it on my own, took the risk, and, despite warning that he could be wrong, I figured he was brilliant, had studied the market with intensity, had been successful thus far, and was actually doing it, not just offering free advice to others about what to do. Besides, I liked Marc, and I wanted a quick and easy profit.

You probably can guess the rest of the story. I'm still

taking the losses off my income taxes, and this happened quite a few years ago. Marc lost most of his fortune, and I lost a good piece of my hard-earned capital. I know that fortunes are made in the stock market. It required taking a risk—one of the essentials of making money. I saw the passion of his attack, and it took perseverance or at least patience to wait out the market for a possible return. The missing ingredient was that my willingness to work was useless to me— once purchased, I had surrendered complete control of making it work. I've made money a number of times by taking a so-so idea and making it work. I had control; it was up to me, win or lose.

Incidentally, I'm happy to say that Marc has since regained a part of his fortune. I'm sad to say that he has left teaching (sad for the students who will not get to experience him), but that's another story. He never gave up on the market and his belief in charting. He has far more persistence than I when it comes to the stock market. I visited with him recently and, to this day, he still charts many stocks. Even though I no longer own a single share of any stock, he has hung in there and, while visiting, he told me of four thousand shares of stock he bought at fifteen cents a share. It went through a reverse split and reduced his number of shares to one thousand but each one of those thousand shares is now worth over eighteen dollars. Persistence has paid off again.

I confess I felt tempted to reinvest as we talked.

Wow, I thought to myself, that's a fantastic profit and no work involved. As my mind heard those tempting voices, it also flashed back to the day I was sold out. It's a case of having even less control than I thought I had. Of course, I knew I had virtually no control over the management of the company. All I controlled, or so I thought, was when to buy and when to sell. Here's what I found out.

I had purchased my seven hundred shares a hundred at a time, on margin; that's where the broker loans you part of the money for the purchase. In margin accounts, your equity must remain at some minimum percentage. That's to keep you from investing with only the broker's money. If you buy one share of a stock for one hundred dollars and you invest sixty dollars of your money and borrow the remaining forty dollars from the broker, then, should the price of that stock fall sixty dollars, you have lost all your investment because the remaining forty dollars is what was borrowed from the broker. If this happens, the broker will require you to put up additional capital. That's known as a margin call.

Well, I had received some margin calls, and each time I sent the broker the additional capital he requested. I knew there was this risk at the time I started investing on margin, and, as I watched the price fall from nineteen to fifteen and from fifteen to ten, I could fairly well anticipate when the calls would be coming. Down it went. I bought more on the way

down, each time telling myself it had finally hit bottom.
I bought more at seven, more still at four. I remember
my last order because of what the broker said to me.
"What do you want more of that sh-- for?" My reply:
"Never mind, Bruce. Just place the order." More
margin calls, answered and met.

Then came one that I had not anticipated. I asked
Bruce to check. He did and, sure enough, I had a
sufficient percentage of equity. The stock was now
about two dollars a share and the computer showed
that I had an equity of about nine hundred dollars. That
was plenty. There was no chance I was investing solely
the broker's money. The whole mess was worth about
fourteen hundred, and about nine hundred of that was
mine and the remaining five hundred was borrowed
from the broker. I was safe, or was I?

Bruce called back. While my percent of equity was
fine, the total dollar value of the equity was too low.
He explained a rule that there must be a minimum
equity of two thousand dollars in any margin account
and mine was obviously a bit short. So, he wanted
additional capital to raise my equity to two thousand
dollars. Foul, said I, that's a low blow. I had never been
told of such a rule and felt it was unfair to tell me of it
now and insist on additional capital. So, I didn't send it.

My next contact came in the mail. It was a notice that
they had sold my seven hundred shares at 1⅞ (the all-
time low) for failure to meet a margin call, the new type
margin call based on the new rule about a two thousand

minimum equity. I wrote to the directors of the New York Stock Exchange and complained, but to no avail. I had now learned how *little* control I really had: none at all, not even control of when to sell.

So, as of this date anyway, I have resisted the temptation to try to find one of those super bargain fifteen-cent stocks that will soon be worth eighteen dollars, and I can tell you that if and when I do give in to the temptation, two things are certain: I'll have compromised my present feelings about control, and I won't be buying from Bruce.

One more warning about control. I know that some franchises are profitable, but many seem to require the purchaser to do everything that he is told, i.e., exercise little control. In effect, such a purchaser may have simply bought himself a job and, in addition, he may be obligating himself to do business with a parent company whose prices are unusually high.

For example, my first car wash was a franchise—notice I say *was*. I soon discovered that I was obliged to buy my soap from the parent firm. Their price was just about double the fair market price. It took some maneuvering, but I soon regained that part of the control. I learned a lesson about having control of what you own.

In summary, control is essential because, without it, your willingness to work can be useless. Control should be maximized—since you own it, you better control it and, insofar as you don't control your business, you really don't own it.

Work When You Feel Like It?

Guideline number two: buy a business with flexible hours.

As a teacher, you are busy teaching during normal business hours with the possible exception of the late afternoons. You no doubt have occasional school-associated duties in the evening. Any sort of business that demands your presence at a certain time every day could be difficult to fit into your schedule. Besides, I've discovered I work far more efficiently when I feel like working. When I have to work but don't really feel like it (that does happen), I can make myself do it, but it's a strain and my efficiency is subnormal. It is way below what it is when I really feel like attacking a piece of work. The pleasure of work is partly in seeing something accomplished and partly in the financial reward, but for me, it is also in seeing it done with facility, i.e., efficiently.

How can there be a business that lets you work when you feel like it? Clearly, there's more to it than that. Any business requires a time commitment, but you look for flexibility. Seek a business that allows you to choose the hours that you will work. My car wash is open twenty-four hours a day, 365 days a year. It needs to be checked daily and, at times, several hours must be spent on maintenance, repairs, improvements, etc.

When this has to be done is flexible, early or late, morning or evening, anytime. Good preventive maintenance and back-up systems will minimize the amount and length of time that is demanded. The additional flexibility comes because it is a partnership and because it has six identical wash bays and three identical vacuum cleaners. That way, we are still operational even if one of the bays or vacuums must be closed down until we can get to it.

There are many businesses with flexible hours. Mail order—fill the orders when you have the time. This is not to imply that you neglect your business for long periods of time. No business can stand much of that. It simply says that you are free to choose to perform these duties and responsibilities at a time that your teaching schedule and family life make most convenient for you.

The vending industry is filled with these sorts of possibilities. One company that I own—Video Vend— has coin-operated TVs in places where people are apt to be waiting or wanting to see TV. We'll put TVs in a few booths in a restaurant. If you want to see the news or a sporting event while you eat or drink coffee, you can. Any kind of vending machine needs some service, but when the servicing is done is flexible. Generally, vending a service (like TV or pinball) requires far less maintenance time than vending a product (like candy or coffee). Throughout the vending industry are multiple opportunities awaiting teachers.

The idea I mentioned about preparing other people's

taxes meets the criteria of flexible hours. In addition to
flexible hours, it's a business that illustrates the age-old
notion of "earn while you learn." It can be learned by
working a tax season or two for one of the large national
firms that do such work. Then, it's off on your own.
Learning a business while working in someone else's
similar business is an easy way to get started. Be
observant, learn all you can about how to operate such
a business, how profitable it is, then use your
willingness to take risks and start one of your own.

I'm certainly not trying to say that if you own a
business, it won't take time—it will. I'll show you how
to find the time in Chapter 5. For now, all I'm saying is
that there are some businesses where the hours are
rather fixed and rigid. Those are probably not well
suited to full-time teachers.

In summary, guideline number two says: Look for a
business with flexible hours.

I Probably Won't Hire You!

The third guideline concerns employees. I indicated
earlier my belief that you'll work much harder in a
business you own than when employed by someone
else. So, if you are now going to own your own
business, what about employees? I have three
suggestions. First, have a business that requires as few
as possible—maybe none. Second, try to have any
necessary employees on some kind of incentive pay.

And third, obtain the services you need on a contract basis rather than by hiring employees.

I've had quite a few summer's experience with painting. We were not just painters, however. We were THE PAINTING TEACHERS. I used to run ads saying, "Have your house painted by people with master's degrees." As a way to start in business, painting in the summer is pretty good.

At first, I worked with another teacher. Soon it became obvious I could make more money by hiring students and teachers and letting them work by the hour while I worked for the profit. At first, I was scared I would not have enough work to keep them busy. I never had a day in ten summers that I was without work, and usually we were booked weeks in advance.

The question then became how to get the employees to produce more, what incentive to use. Somehow fixed hourly wages didn't seem to provide much real incentive. The employees were working, but they didn't seem to be attacking the jobs and I wanted an attack, not just slow, steady painting.

I began working on what was to later be referred to by the crew as "another one of his famous deals." We'd be halfway finished with a house and I'd see two days' work left. I'd say, "Look, you guys, I'll finish the entire east end by myself. All you have to do are the three other sides. There's one of me and six of you. You start now and I'll pay everybody till nine o'clock tonight— but you can quit as soon as you've finished." There would be haggling, but they loved the challenge. Win or lose, it was more fun. I often clinched the deal by offering to buy lunch the next day for the entire crew at Snead's (well known for their delicious barbecue). Off they would go—it was a new crew—attacking now instead of just painting, telling each other to hurry and keep busy rather than having me tell them. Often, they'd end up having to help me finish my side and they never really seemed to mind too much. They could razz hell out of me because they had beat me, and that was worth the time it took to help finish my end.

At the end of the summer, I'd always throw a big party for all the painters and they'd recall laughingly how they'd gotten a certain house done by seven o-clock, got paid until nine, and got a free lunch at Snead's besides. It was more fun for all of us, plus it meant more profit for me and good business, too.

The point is that everyone works best when challenged and when there's a team effort. The incentive is there that's missing when it's just hourly wages.

An alternate incentive is a percentage of the profits. It's sometimes more difficult to work out the details. I'd usually keep the students on hourly salaries and give the teachers an hourly salary plus some fixed percentage of profits. In any business, it's the profit that is the incentive to work harder and more efficiently.

In one summer, I had as many as twelve working together. We were working on a fairly large commercial job and were behind schedule. One house we had a contract to do was supposed to have been done the week before. The owner had called and I explained the delay as best I could and gave a promise to start that week. It was Wednesday, and it became obvious our commercial job would take us well into the next week. Thursday after lunch, I had the crew load up the gear we'd need and off we went. Thirteen is a few too many to paint a house efficiently. When we arrived, the lady of the house called her husband at his office to let him know we were finally getting started. She told us he would be home early to check with us. It was not a small house. In any case, as he drove in his driveway about 4:30 P.M., we were loading up our gear. In fact, most of the crew had gone already. He was a bit shocked to be told after his lunch we were starting and four hours later to find us done. Admittedly, that's not the efficient way to do it—we got in each other's way at times. Still, there was quite a thrill to see an entire house painted that fast. It was an incentive—just to see how fast we could do one—to be able to go home that evening and say, "You won't believe this, but we started on this guy's big house after lunch and we had the sucker done before he got home from work."

The right group of employees can be fun to work with. Still, employees can cause problems. The employer taxes are stiff and rising. My share of the taxes amounted to about 8 percent of payroll. I had schedules to record and constant questions to answer that cut into the time I could keep a brush in my hand.

Slowly, I developed my present attitude: As few employees as possible, incentive pay for employees if you must have some, and services by contract.

At my car washes, I have contract snow removal, contract lawn service, contract clean-up service, contract sewer service, and contract trash service. I have recently put one of the car washes on a contract management service. I think contract management carries the notion about as far as it can be carried, but so far it seems to be working well. In my coin-operated TV business, I have contract repair service and have contracted for their weekly maintenance. Each week, a man I have a contract with has agreed to clean the sets, test and adjust them, replace any defective ones, empty the money, and deposit it in the bank.

These contractual arrangements avoid all payroll taxes. Of course, they are a legitimate business expense and acceptable to the IRS, and they minimize the amount of time I need to spend in supervision. The duties are clearly spelled out ahead of time—as clearly as possible, though they change as the business changes. The pay is a fixed sum or a fixed percent of the gross or net income. Two such contracts I have are with other teachers, two with relatives of my partners, one with a former student. All of these people I can trust and knew for quite some time before I chose to offer them contracts. The remaining contracts are with people in that field of business, like the trash service and the TV set repairing. The arrangements seem to work well and avoid the usual problems one hears about from people who own businesses with many employees.

So guideline number three: as few employees as possible. But if employees are necessary, give them incentives, but minimize the number of actual employees by obtaining the services you need under contract.

Nothing for Something

Guideline four: Get something for your money. I know it sounds silly, too obvious, but some people pay for the privilege of doing business with others. In looking at any business, be very careful of such fees. These are the charges for start-up. Often, some inventory is included but probably not enough to justify the fee. If you don't get something with real market value, it could be a phony. It's at least questionable in many cases, and I view these types of businesses with a very watchful and suspicious eye.

Guideline number four should be clear: don't pay for the privilege of doing business with others.

Cash, Man, Cash!

Guideline number five concerns cash flow versus equity accrual. Cash flow is the amount of money that a business produces in spendable profit. Equity accrual is the (hopefully) increasing value of a business obtainable only if it were to be sold. As a teacher, you need extra income now. The sort of business that will pay a nice return years from now is not what you're looking for. If you could put $100 a month in a savings account (at today's rates) and if you could do so every month for fifteen years, then you can draw out $100 a month for the rest of your life—in fact, forever. The interest for the fifteen-year period and the money you have deposited will be sufficient to generate an interest income of about $1,200 a year. But you can't start collecting for fifteen years or maybe a little sooner depending on the rates. In any case, it's too long to wait. That may be fine for retirement, but you need income now, a business that shows a monthly profit.

That calls for a cash business. Each time you sell some product or service, there should be a profit that you can spend just like you spend your teaching salary. In the days before double-digit inflation, one could purchase a second house, rent it for a bit more than the payments, and have it paid off in twenty years. Then the rent (less taxes, repairs, etc.) became profit. But there was the long wait. You were slowly accruing an equity, but there was little cash flow. Today, when real estate is going up so fast, the wait can be shortened. You can sell a few years after you buy and probably have a nice profit.

We tried the real estate game with modest success. My partner in the Christmas tree business was a full-time real estate salesman. He knew about the long wait if you buy, rent, and then sell a house. He discovered how to have cash flow as well as how to minimize the wait.

We bought a house that had been converted into small apartments and rooms. We bought from the owner for minimum down, and she was willing to carry the financing. We bought in an old neighborhood where some of the poorer houses were being torn down and where the zoning had been changed from single-family to multiple, and we bought a house with a big lot. We were willing to work—fixing it up a little, maintaining it, and keeping it rented. We found that with all the apartments and rooms rented (including the converted detached garage), the rental income was more than triple the payments. As a single-family residence, this house would have rented at a $175-a-month maximum. It was too big and too expensive to heat for most families who would be willing to live in that neighborhood. Once converted and rented, it was producing quite a cash flow for us, especially in the warmer months. Within less than three years, the neighborhood was alive with the apartment boom. The big lot was now worth more than the house. We sold at a modest profit and soon the house was gone and a new 18-unit apartment building was in its place. It had given us all three: good cash flow, a little equity accrual, and some appreciation.

Real estate is full of possibilities for teachers, but

keep your eye on cash flow. That's what teachers need: cash now. In looking at any business, find out how much cash you can expect to take out and how soon. Fifteen years is a long time to wait.

So there are my five guidelines. You need control. You need flexible hours. You want as few employees as possible—hopefully none. You can't afford to pay for the pleasure of doing business with someone, and it's cash *now* that you're after.

Now I'll tell you how to get the money to get started.

4

On Acquisition of Capital

Here are five ways to acquire capital. Some are tough; but some are not as tough as you might think.

Moonbeams

Moonlight. Get a second job and save the money. You're worth what you save, not what you earn. Put the money aside as risk capital. I've carried mail, worked as a draftsman, janitor, retail clerk, etc. It's a time to learn and save. Tell yourself it's not your money, put it in a separate account, but by all means save it. Spending will always rise to meet income, but if you let it do that, you are doomed to two jobs forever. It's a tough way to acquire capital, but it's a way.

In addition to acquiring capital, a part-time job, if carefully chosen or even found by accident, will provide useful training and experience for a business of your own. One of my college summers was spent working in a small sheet metal shop. I was working as a draftsman and when there was not enough drafting work to keep me busy, I'd work in the fabrication shop. It was of no great use to me until years later, but when our coin-operated TV scheme needed to have cases and coin slides fabricated, I knew how to get started and where to go for help. I had chosen the job because it was what was available for summer work, but the knowledge I gained was useful many years later.

So, choose a part-time job that's in a field of interest to you, and learn all you can about the business while saving for one of your own.

Moonlighting is a tough way to acquire capital, but it can be a profitable learning experience at the same time. Besides, if it takes long, hard hours of moonlighting to acquire the needed capital, you're apt to do whatever's needed to keep from losing it. So when you start your own business with it, those memories of how tough it was to earn and save the capital will be forceful reminders to work hard and hang in there when it gets tough, lest you lose your capital and have all that moonlighting go for naught. Anything that was hard to get will probably be taken good care of.

Borrow from Yourself

Borrow on the cash value of your life insurance. If you have been paying life insurance premiums on other than term insurance, you may have quite an asset. You can borrow the money thus saved from your insurance company. These loans don't have a fixed repayment schedule. If you die, the insurance company will deduct the loan from the proceeds of the policy. Often the rate of interest you pay is lower than bank rates. I think of it as borrowing from myself and have done so to help start two of my ventures. A word of caution here: since there's no fixed repayment schedule, it's very easy to postpone repayment even when the business is healthy and you could afford to repay. That's no crime, of course, but it has happened to me and I know it means that asset won't be available the next time I need it. So, once you can, start paying it back.

The Old Homestead

If you have owned a home for just a few years (even if you made a minimum down payment), you probably have quite an equity. In our area, real estate values have been going up 8 to 15 percent a year. A house that cost $25,000 three years ago could easily be worth $35,000. If you have such a house, you can refinance it and have a bushel full of cash. Your payments will be somewhat higher, but it will give you the capital you need to start. If you do not want to refinance the house, you can take a second mortgage on it. One of my partners recently refinanced his house to have the investment capital he wanted. He'd paid about $30,000 for the house about six years earlier and had made some improvements over the years. When he refinanced it, he got almost $40,000 in cash, and that was after paying off the original mortgage of about $18,000. He had paid $30,000, and six years later, it was worth almost $80,000.

Another partner has established a line of credit where he can borrow up to $10,000 any time he wants. He used a second mortgage as the collateral for the loan and now is the sole owner of Applied Physics. He's a physics teacher at a local college and, in his company, uses his knowledge of electronics to design and fabricate all sorts of specialized electronic controls.

Borrow from Others

Borrowing from banks is always a possibility. My view of borrowing from banks is that it's sometimes necessary, seldom easy, and has never been pleasant for me. I recall one situation when I wanted to borrow from a bank. Our company that manufactures coin-operated TV sets had hastily decided to increase our inventory by one-hundred sets. We needed an additional $7,500 to pay for the soon-to-arrive C.O.D. shipment. The choices were for each partner to make an additional investment or borrow the money from our bank.

I called the bank and the banker was busy. He could see me next week, three days after I needed the money. Finally, with persistence, I got to see him the same day (big deal). I explained our need: $7,500 for ninety days, secured by a $5,000 certificate of deposit and the signatures of both partners. He told me that would "leave him open on $2,500." He frowned, saying "I don't know, I don't like being open on $2,500." Now he was saying that to a man who had banked there for over fifteen years, a man with a net worth well into six figures—over a third of that in cash—and who was only one of the two people who were going to sign the note. He knew from the financial statements we keep on file there that our combined monthly incomes were over double the $2,500 he was worried about being "open" on. He made us the loan, but I left there with basically the same feeling I've gotten from bankers time and time again: I'm a little kid begging for an almost unreasonable favor from big daddy. I don't treat my customers that way and don't like to be treated that way.

I've learned a few techniques for dealing with bankers to maximize the likelihood of getting the loan you want.

Give them loads of time. Don't seem anxious. Let them know you have plenty of time to shop around for a loan and they will have ample time to decide.

Give them the proposal for the loan in writing and, with it, the things you know they'll want: type and amount of collateral, term and amount of loan, start-up costs for your business, projected balance sheets, and a prediction of monthly income and outgo.

Ask about the interest rate. It can be hypothetical. If you approve the loan, what will the rate be? It's good information for you—where else would you hesitate to ask the price of an article?

Keep on good terms with more than one bank and

somehow, let each one know you're on good terms with the others. Banking is competitive like any other business, and it's good to let a banker think you'll go right to his closest competitor if he refuses the loan. In addition, it can happen that one bank actually wants more loans of a certain type and another has all of that type they can handle.

If they refuse a loan, ask why and press on till you get a specific answer. The first reason given is very apt to be vague. Ask just which part of your written proposal they did not like or thought was too risky, then listen to what they say. If it's really a specific answer, it may tell you how to rewrite the proposal for the next bank or it may show you a risk you hadn't considered. Then ask for a written letter of refusal. You'll see why this could be useful in a page or two.

I've said it before and I'll say it again. The basic attitude of banks is: prove to us you don't need the money and we'll loan it to you. So be as confident, self-assured, and positive as you can be. When I get that feeling that I'm being treated like a little kid asking for a favor, I quickly remind myself it's almost certain I make a good bit more money than the clown who's sitting across the desk from me.

Pay them back early every once in a while. It sends them the message you need to have them hear. You have money and no longer need theirs.

In dealing with banks, I suspect your chances are better with a small, rural bank than a large, big city one.

In the banks that I've tried to borrow from in our city, the officer usually says he will present the request to the loan committee. That means there won't just be one person looking for reasons not to help you get started; there will be a group of people. Since I believe finding reasons not to do something is one of the easiest things in the world to do, I'm not surprised that when a whole group tries to do it together, they're going to refuse nine times out of ten.

In a small-town bank, it could be different. The man you talk to may be able to decide without a committee. In addition, he may even own the bank and may remember how tough it was getting started and so be more willing to take a risk, or he may remember his favorite third grade teacher and see this as a chance to help a teacher like good old Miss Gimwitch. Even if he can't make you the loan, he may know individuals he can send you to who would consider making the loan.

I mentioned before that if the bank refuses, ask for a letter of refusal. This could be useful in obtaining a loan through the Small Business Administration (SBA). It's a federal agency whose purpose is to help small businesses.

The SBA can guarantee your loan (up to 90 percent) when a banker thinks it's too risky for him to go it alone. These are known as participation agreements and the bank provides the money while the SBA backs the loan. There's a former Georgia peanut farmer, now rather famous, who got one of these participation loans to help his business.

The SBA also can make direct loans. It will only do so if you have been turned down by a bank or sometimes two. That's why you ask the bank for a letter saying so if they refuse to give you a loan. The interest rate on these loans is usually well below bankers' rates, but they're not easy to get, and it may take six months or longer from time of first application until you actually get the money. That's one of the joys of dealing with the bureaucracy, so be prepared for red tape if you're going to the SBA.

In addition to participation loans and direct loans, the SBA has quite a few free or inexpensive publications that might be of help. Two of the free ones are called *Checklist for Going into Business* and SBA *Business Loans.* These are usually available at the local SBA office, along with a list of the ones that can be purchased from the Government Printing Office in Washington, D.C.

SBA publications have been a great help to many small businesses and yet, reading their publications seemed to me to be discouraging. At least I'm glad I didn't read them before I was reasonably successful with businesses of my own. It reminded me of what I would do to a freshman algebra class if I spent the first week asking them hundreds of questions about algebra. They're just starting the course, they know they don't know algebra, and it would discourage them to be asked many questions they couldn't be expected to answer. The SBA publications did that to me. They created more doubts than they relieved. It seems almost anti-intellectual to oppose asking many, many questions. A few are essential, but I found too many to be discouraging. It seemed to me to focus too much attention on the reasons (excuses) not to go into business. All of us can find plenty of reasons not to do it, and getting asked too many questions just seemed to supply more doubts.

Banks and the SBA are not the only possible sources of money. Credit unions are a possibility. If you're a member of a teacher's credit union or a church union, you have two more possible sources. All the aforementioned sources are in business to make loans, and besides these more or less conventional sources, there's always a possibility you could borrow from friends or relatives.

I know there are a couple of old sayings about lending: "lend a dollar and lose a friend" and "neither a borrower nor a lender be." True, there is a chance that borrowing money can be a strain on friendship. To minimize the strain, be sure that all facts concerning the loan are spelled out in writing. I have borrowed thousands of dollars from friends and still owe about $3,000 to one friend. I've loaned hundreds of dollars to friends and am still owed some of it. So far, so good—the friends are still friends. So those old admonitions about lending should be taken with a grain of salt. It has worked for me.

I'm not as well acquainted with borrowing from
relatives (or lending money to them). When my father
was living, I'd borrow a few dollars from him once in a
while, but I confess it made me uncomfortable. He
would certainly not have expected me to stop eating to
get the money to pay him back. The problem was I'd
have felt guilty each bite I took if I had failed to repay
him. It was reassuring to know that he had modest
savings that, as an absolute last resort or in a dire crisis, I
could borrow. In fact, he'd have given it to me if I
absolutely had to have it, but I was quite hesitant to do
so. I guess it depends on how much you need, for how
long you'll need it, how much money the relatives have,
and, mostly, on what sort of relationship you have with
them. Regardless of the relationship, I'd want it all
down in writing to do all I could to minimize the chance
of later recriminations.

So, borrowing is the fourth way to acquire the start-
up money you need. Borrowing from banks can be
unpleasant, but there are ways to increase your chances
of getting a bank to loan you the money. If banks are no
help, there are other sources in the lending business
and, beyond those, there are friends and relatives.

Cars, Trading, Doing It Yourself, Free TVs

There are four ways to acquire capital by keeping a
good bit more of what you make as a teacher. (This is
my favorite method 'cause it's painless and fun.) The

first is to buy John Olson's book, *How to Make Money Owning Your Car*. Car expense is a major budget item. Depreciation is a major car expense. Olson has put down on paper what I had been doing for years. He tells you how to make money on the cars you own. It sounds crazy. Sell the car for more than I paid for it? Right. Just figure up the depreciation on the last three or four cars you've owned. How much did you pay for the car and how much did you really get for it when you traded? If the depreciation isn't $1,000 a year, you're exceptional. If it's under $500, that's very rare. In any case, it's a lot of money to a teacher. Olson doesn't just tell you how to cut down on depreciation; he tells you how to reverse the situation. Sell for more than you paid. My last five sales were:

- Paid $600, sold for $3,500.
- Paid $800, sold for $1,475.
- Paid $200, sold for $1,350.
- Paid $600, sold for $1,000.
- Paid $400, sold for $850.

A few of these required extensive investment, so the figures are not net profit but, on all five as a group, I lost not one cent to depreciation in ten years and I drove them over 100,000 miles. I know it sounds too good to be true. Read the book. Here's where you can order it: John R. Olson, 2020 Girard Avenue South, Minneapolis, Minnesota 55405.

A second technique is to trade your services for those you need. Mothers who trade baby-sitting services by

watching each others' children have known about this
for years. How about trading tutoring services for the
plumber's kids in exchange for his plumbing repairs.
Ditto for the local car mechanic. It saves on taxes as
well as expenses and is one more way to keep a bit more
of what you earn.

Third is to do it yourself. As a teacher, you know
about libraries. You probably have easy access to one
and may have a librarian in your school who will
borrow or buy any book that you want to read. Books
will tell you how to do many things. Read them and do it
yourself. Besides books, you have fellow teachers in
shop, auto mechanics, etc. Ask them to help you. If you
teach at the secondary level, you have access to cheap
labor (students) and probably a fair idea which ones
would be good workers. When our house needed an
addition, I read a book, bought materials (at a discount)
from a former student of mine, hired some students to
help me, and went at it. There were some trying
moments and I finally did subcontract some of the
work, but the total cost was probably less than half what
it would have been if I had had the whole thing done for
me.

And fourth is to complain and sue if necessary. When
something you purchase is unsatisfactory, let the seller
know about it. I still watch a color TV that was given to
me by a major manufacturer for one of his earlier sets
that was three years old. The original one had thirty-
five service calls in the three years I owned it. I was not
too upset because all the calls were covered by a
service policy and were not costing me anything but

the annoyance. I wrote the manufacturer a somewhat joking letter about what it must be costing him to service such a dud. They understood, and despite the fact the set was three years old, they replaced it with a new one. They charged me $50. I sold the old set for $125. When complaining, move quickly to the top and persevere.

Be reasonable but insistent. I had a disagreement with a new car dealer about warranty coverage. Dealer said no, zone office said no, Detroit said no. It cost me twelve dollars to sue the highest local official of the company in small claims court. The day before the trial, they all said yes. I felt they were just testing me because their experience tells them that most people will give up after three nos. Perseverance wins.

That's it for acquiring capital. You earn and save it (moonlighting), borrow from yourself (insurance), transfer equities to cash (refinance house), borrow from banks, credit unions, friends, or keep a bit more of what you earn (cars, trading, do it yourself, or complaining).

5

The Details of Doing It - Starting Your Own Business

How to Finance It

First, you need to calculate how much capital you have available. This is a matter of net worth—that amount of cash you would have left if everything you own was sold at fair market value and all your debts and bills were paid.

Once you determine your net worth, divide it into the part which is easily and inexpensively available and which does not require a fixed pay-back schedule. That includes your savings, cash value in life insurance, and items easily convertible to cash like stocks, bonds, and savings certificates. Add it up, and, if you're a typical teacher, it's not apt to be much. If it's nothing, then start moonlighting and saving, or be ready to borrow or refinance your house.

Next, determine what you could borrow on your house or other assets or from any source including relatives, friends, and fellow teachers.

When my partner in the Christmas tree business and I

decided that we would start a car wash, we each had about $1,000 to invest. That meant that we were about $20,000 short of what we needed. The search began at banks and was very discouraging. Because it was a new industry (coin-operated car washes were less than a year old at the time), it meant high risk. I still recall asking my wife's uncle, a very wealthy and influential banker, where to borrow the money. He quickly told me that his bank had taken a very careful look at the industry and that there was no way it could work. He even added he was doing me a favor by not loaning me the money—that he was saving me from financial disaster. Of course, he didn't know that I had decided to do it and was in the midst of a passionate search for the money. I was going to get it somewhere or die, and he was one of those negative thinkers. I'm afraid most bankers are.

The search went on. Neither of us was willing to ask our parents (both of whom had modest savings) for a loan. That may have been a mistake, but we were too proud and independent, though I'd no doubt have done it as an absolute last resort. One of my fellow teachers (Marc Murdock) had clear title to a farm he'd inherited and was willing to become a partner by putting up his $1,000 to match ours, then loan us the remaining $19,000 by borrowing on his farm. He would be a silent partner. We agreed to pay 10 percent interest (very high for the time) but worked out a somewhat unusual repayment plan. I believe this plan can serve as

a model for starting a business, and I've used similar
ones since then.

The two active partners owed the silent partner
$19,000. He agreed to be repaid as follows. Each
month, he was to receive his interest payment and 50
percent of the operational profit to be applied to the
principal. The two active partners each got 25 percent
of the operational profit for the work they were doing
to manage the car wash. Such a repayment plan gives
immediate spendable income to the people who are
actively working. That's good incentive to get them to
do their job well. It also tends to protect them from
further cash outlay because if there is really a lean
month, there is no fixed payment to be made on the
principal. It might seem that few investors would be
willing to do that, but realize what Marc was getting:
his 10 percent interest (quite an incentive for us to
repay because it was a high rate for the time) plus one-
third of the equity in a business in which his total
investment was $1,000. And he wasn't doing a thing to
get it.

We bought a second car wash a few years later, and
the silent partner became active. The three of us finally
split up. Marc got one car wash, and my active partner
and I got the other. After operating his by himself for
about a year and a half, Marc sold it to us. Our track
record was established by then and we were able to
buy it with minimum down payment.

The point is that we were willing to take the risk, to

do the work, and to pursue the problem of financing until we got it worked out. Making the decision to do it, no matter the cost, got it done. The project was at the limit of what we could attempt with our capital. You can't usually buy a $100,000 business for $50 down, not when you're getting started.

So, calculate how much capital you have or set a definite goal in a definite time for acquiring it. Then look for a business in that price range. As a rule of thumb, 10 percent is minimum cash. That may leave you on thin ice, but depending on how quick the return is and how high the cash flow is, that can be enough.

In buying any small business, owner financing is often available. You'll probably find as a teacher you have a good chance of convincing an owner to carry the loan. Remember, folks tend to have fond memories of some teacher or school. They may be willing to go an extra mile for you because you're a teacher. People know teachers are poorly paid and so sometimes are willing to give them a break. Besides, most people who own small businesses remember how tough it was to get started. There's a good chance someone helped them and so they might do the same, especially for a teacher.

Now, you know how much you've got or how much you're going to save or borrow. You're willing to risk all of it or a certain amount of it, so you're ready for the next step. Even with the money, how do you find the time? Teaching is a full-time job, isn't it?

How to Find the Time

I have often been asked, "How do you run all your businesses and teach, too?" I suspect sometimes the questioner has visions of much more elaborate business ventures than I am actually involved in. In the back of our house, I have a small (less than 40 square feet) office. If I ever want to get fancy and have a sign made for my door, I'll put on it: General Offices of Video Vend, Home Office of Associated T.V. Products, Executive Offices for CFM Car Wash, Warehouse, Shipping and Receiving for CFG Car Washes, Purchasing, Personnel, and Maintenance Departments, Communication Center and Conference Room for all of the above. Then when someone enters and finds he can stand in the center and reach all of the four walls, he'll know why some businesses sound like a lot more than they really are.

So how to find the time? As a teacher, you know the school calendar. Your school is probably open 175 to 180 days a year. There are about 245 working days in a year. That means that I am free almost 30 percent of the normal working days. That's time to be used for business.

In our school, we get one period a day free for planning, four minutes between classes, and a duty-free, thirty-minute lunch period. I see some teachers while away their free periods day after day. I'm serious about teaching. All my tests are always corrected and returned the next day, and in twenty years, I've never

given a class a study period because I was not
prepared. I guess I subscribe to the belief that if you
want to get something done, ask a busy person to do it.
We each have the same twenty-four hours in any given
day. I've found I can check quite a few quizzes in the
four minutes between classes. It is a matter of
efficiency. I am able to do my teaching work, give the
students who ask for it extra help, and almost always be
finished by 4:00 P.M. It is a rare day that I bring work
home. I use the time that I have as efficiently as I can. I
like to end my day and be home by 6:30 P.M. I know
that leaves two-and-a-half hours a day for business
activity, and I use those efficiently, also.

You have the same sort of opportunity. The business
should have flexible hours because you may prefer
mornings or evenings to late afternoons for working.
But as a teacher, you do have the time if you will use it
efficiently. I also use some part of my Saturdays, but I
do not suggest that you devote more than twenty hours
a week to business and fifteen would be preferable.

You've got some money, some time, you're willing to
take a chance, willing to do the work, and ready to hang
in there. But which business?

What's Your Pleasure?

It's a matter of what you like and are interested in and
a matter of what's available in your price range while
still meeting most of the aforementioned guidelines

(control, hours, employees, real value, and cash flow). So, first figure out your interests and likes. It may be sufficient to eliminate those areas that you genuinely dislike. Obviously, I can't tell you what you like or are interested in. I can only tell you that in the long run, being in something you like and find interesting will be much easier than its opposite. I'd rate it as important but not critical.

Psychologists claim that the main reason people work is the need for achievement, that money is secondary. More people quit work because of a lack of feeling of achievement and not getting along with co-workers than because of low pay or offers of jobs that pay more. For teachers, this has quite an implication. If your teaching job meets the first reasons for working— need for achievement and meaningful relations with coworkers—then owning a business while teaching can enable you to focus more attention on your profits. The need for achievement and relationships will, of course, be met to some additional extent, but the principal reason for this endeavor is money. Since the usual reasons for working are now secondary, the focus on money can be primary, and that's mighty good for business. The reversal of the reasons for working is possible only because you're a teacher and in business, too.

You'll develop a fondness for and an interest in any business which is making you good money. It will be all the easier if it is one you like and find interesting from

the beginning. Just avoid the one that you can't stand
and don't spend a lot of time and energy on this phase.
It could become a real source of procrastination. In
some of the books I've read about business, there's
often a suggestion that one get started by taking what is
now a hobby and doing it for profit. Thus the coin
collector becomes the coin dealer or the dancer
becomes the dance instructor or the bicyclist starts a
bike shop.

I have some doubts about the notion of turning a
hobby into a business. I like the aspect that would have
you in a business you like and have found interesting
as a hobby. The reservation I have is the change that
will happen to you when what you used to do strictly
for enjoyment is now going to be done for profit. To
me, the two reasons could conflict.

I collect old cars for a hobby. It's a hobby that in
recent years has attracted many investors and I suspect
there are now many "hobbyists" who are simply in it
for the money. I've been tempted and have resisted.
Many of the decisions I've made about cars have been
based strictly on what I felt like doing. It would
certainly be bad car business to search for hours in junk
yards to find a piece of chrome that's in slightly better
condition than the one that's presently on the side of
one of my convertibles. It could easily take hours to
find such a piece and hours more to change it, and it
would not improve the value of the car by much at all.
But to me it's fun and it's satisfying each time I look

at the new chrome that's a little better than it was before. Bad from a business point of view, yet good from the point of view of my own mental health. The "car nuts" know the satisfaction, and I suspect other hobbyists know of similar enjoyments.

When building model ships, knitting sweaters, or playing bridge, it's the enjoyment of the hobby that's fun and healthy. To do exactly the same things but with a constant eye on profitability could very easily compromise the fun. Imagine trying to evaluate the increase in the value of the car versus the time and expense of getting a better chrome piece. Financially it's out of the question, and having to make such calculations would somehow spoil the fun for me.

Hobbies are good for mental health. Trying to blend in profits and maintain the hobby status is tricky. Implying that what has been a good hobby will be a good business is questionable. There's a good bit more to business than there is to hobbying. If I ever should decide to take up "old cars" as a business, one of my first prerequisites will be a new hobby. I doubt that I could mix the two without compromising both. I guess it has been done successfully and yet keeping them separate works better for me.

So before you try to turn your hobby into a business, at least ask yourself if it will still really be a hobby. If you do decide to make it into a business, have a new hobby waiting. If it's still as much fun as a business and hobby, please let me know how I can devote

twelve hours to locating and installing a chrome piece
that ups the value of the car by $10 (maybe) and still
feel like it's good business ('cause I know already it's
good hobbying.)

Now to what's available. How to find out? I rely on
the business opportunity sections of papers. I read our
local daily, a few of the small neighborhood weeklies,
and sometimes the national financial papers. I like to
find out what's happening on the West Coast because
there seems to be more of a willingness there to try new
ventures.

Besides the papers, I watch the streets. Each time I
see a foundation being started, I'm curious to know
what it's going to be. That's how I found out about coin-
operated car washes before most of the country ever
heard of such a thing.

Some firms specialize in selling businesses. I've never
bought one from one of these firms but I have
discussed several with them. Once they find out you're
looking for a business and are serious about getting one,
they will contact you whenever they have something
that might suit your needs.

Another resource for finding out what's available
that I am going to mention is a fairly new one to me. I've
seen a few ads for trade shows that are designed to be
forums for the starting of new businesses, and so when
there was one here, I went and took a look.

There were forty-one booths offering a wide variety
of business opportunities, and each of these booths was

staffed by one, two, or three salespersons. These were people who were enthusiastic about what they were doing. That's contagious and can serve as a help if you are somewhat hesitant about starting on your own. Of course, these same enthusiastic people were salespersons (working on commission as a rule) and, that's their job, so be aware. Sort out the sales pitch from the facts. One way to do this is to ask the person if he personally operates one of these sideline businesses in addition to selling them to others. If he does not, you can draw your own conclusion. Maybe a better question is, did he ever?

In order to help sort out the facts from the salesmanship, as I approached the various booths (I chose to go at a time when I thought it would be least busy), I told each salesperson that my interest was academic, that I was a teacher, and that I was at the show to see what educational benefits I might obtain for myself or my students. I felt that was 95 percent honest, though sufficiently vague as to mean damn near anything. I wanted to make clear I was not a prospect for their business at this time but would like some information about it.

That seemed to relax the salespeople and, as long as they weren't busy, they were glad to chat (such shows must be very dull for the salespeople when they don't have potential clients to talk to and some seemed to me almost anxious to chat). Once again, telling them I was a teacher seemed like an icebreaker (fond memories of old Miss Gimwitch?). While talking to three different salespeople, there was an implication from them they understood I did not make much money and I suspected their knowing they made more than teachers put them at ease.

Once the ice was broken, I got more straight information. One said, "Well, then, I won't pitch my product to you." I felt relief. Being told about something can be nice; having it pitched at you seems to imply you better be ready to duck or catch or you're going to be hit with it. Even in just telling me about it, contagious enthusiasm showed through and I like that. Some were quite up-front about capital requirements, even had signs posted. Others I had to ask.

In less than three hours, I observed eight varieties of vending machines including one that takes your blood pressure and for fifty cents (maybe a dollar) prints the results and "hands" it to you. There was a booth which sold established businesses from all over the country and of all different types. There were opportunities to sell health foods, oil paintings, pots and pans, batteries, cleaning products, makeup, book covers, mopeds, and pontoon boats. There were five opportunities in the printing industry; from business cards to large plastic signs, printing was well represented. There was a new process for removing chips from windshields, and the salesperson there said their formula was not patented and never would be. Like the formula for Coca-Cola, it would remain a secret and unpatented for fear of being copied. There was an opportunity to become a manufacturer of fiberglass sinks, a coater of asphalt driveways, or a renewer of old doors. You could have gotten into the car rental businesss, the rug-cleaning business, the publishing business, or the animal-raising business.

A few salespeople were too much. I'm skeptical as hell when somebody tells me there is a guaranteed 100 percent return per year. I know it's possible, but look out. It's almost certain to be 100 percent return and zero dollars per hour for your time.

I left the show feeling it was $2.50 (admission price) very well spent. It was at least as entertaining as the last movie I paid three bucks to see and probably more so. But beyond that, I had observed forty-one booths or exhibits. I checked over my notes and found four or five which, if I were actively seeking another business, would be worthy of more study. Some of these appealed to me because of personal taste—things I like and appreciate and have fun with. Others were of no interest to me. I do not want to raise animals of any kind. I don't like 'em. Still, raising animals was there and for you biology teachers who are fascinated by such critters, there's apparently money to be made with the likes of chinchillas.

As an efficient means for viewing many and varied ways to make money, such a show seems hard to beat and the salespeople you meet seem like models of enthusiasm. Along with the information, at its very worst, it's cheap entertainment. My only reservation is that I was not talking to actual owners of operational businesses. They could only predict what would happen if I bought. Nonetheless, I would recommend such shows.

As a final assist in choosing a small business, it would be interesting, though by no means decisive, to know what the pros say about success and failure. *Money* magazine polled twenty-six such pros and asked them to select candidates for success and failure from their list of the eighty-one most common small businesses. Successful meant apt to survive more than five years.

Before naming them, I must express a reservation or two. These are predictions of experts. After quite a few successful years in my own small business, I took one of those tests designed to predict if I had the qualities to be an entrepreneur. It predicted I'd better either have "a superb business idea or a lot of money" if I was going to be successful in my own business. I had been successful without either! What I do have is willingness to take risks, willingness to work, and perseverance. So the predictions of experts are interesting and fallible.

My second reservation about such a list is that, while it refers to small business, some of these don't seem small to me. With those reservations, here are the ten that *Money* predicted most likely to fail during the first five years of operation:

1. Local laundries and dry cleaners
2. Used car dealerships

3. Gas stations
4. Local trucking firms
5. Restaurants
6. Infants' clothing stores
7. Bakeries
8. Machine shops
9. Grocery and meat stores
10. Car washes

The ten *Money* predicted most likely to succeed were:

1. Building materials stores
2. Auto tire and accessories stores
3. Liquor stores
4. Sports and recreational clubs
5. Funeral homes and crematories
6. Seed and garden supply stores
7. Sporting goods manufacturers
8. Engineering, laboratory, and scientific equipment manufacturers
9. Hardware stores
10. Office supplies and equipment stores

Some made the best-ten list because they're thought to be resistant to recessions, some because of increased numbers of do-it-yourselfers. Some made the ten-worst list because of stiff competition and some because of increased governmental regulations. I think it's an interesting list of predictions, particularly interesting to me since my two newest businesses (car washes) are on the ten-worst list. Of course, had I seen the article before going into them, I'd have gone ahead anyway. It would have been all the more challenging and all the more fun to make a success of one of the worst. I doubt if Ray Kroc, founder of McDonald's Corporation, would have been deterred by such predictions.

Where to Locate

If it is to be a business operated out of a fixed location, then try to find one close to home. I'll never understand why some folks will spend an hour driving to their job and another getting home. Two hours a day is unreasonable travel time for busy people. I operate businesses on less than two hours a day, so I surely can't afford that kind of time getting to and from them. If business is not close to home, then consider moving home close to the business, but either way, minimize your travel time. It's inefficient and expensive to drive long distances just to get to the work.

When to Take the Plunge

That's a consideration that can be viewed from two sides. The first is that you'll have more time in the summer, so that may be a good time for you to start. The second factor is that some businesses do better at certain times of the year. It's best to start one of those at a time when it will do best. Some, like fireworks and

Christmas trees, are strictly seasonal. Some, like amusement parks and swimming pools, operate only in the summers. If you want a one-shot item so that you can see how you will do, then try Christmas trees, fireworks, a summer painting business, lawn service, etc. In fact, the best time to start is when the urge strikes you. If you keep waiting for just the perfect moment, you'll be apt to drag on indecisively. You'll keep reconsidering and reconsidering. Once you feel ready, do it. That's the best time to start.

Specific Questions to Ask About Any Business You're Considering

- How much real profit did it show last year? Ask to see the tax returns; they are the best record. The business could be doing better than the tax return shows (the owner could be skimming some of the profits), but it is not apt to be doing worse than they show.
- Look at possible trends in the improvement of profits. Which way do they seem to be going? A failing business can be difficult to turn around. I'd rather pay more and get one that has a record of growth and increasing profits.
- How many hours' work did it take on the part of the owner to make the profit shown in the tax returns?
- Get a total focus on the cost. There's more to the cost than just the price, particularly if owner financing

is involved. The second car wash we bought seemed to be priced a bit on the high side, but the terms were ideal. The owner was willing to finance two-thirds of it over a ten-year period, and the interest was the same rate that his bank was paying him on his savings. That meant that the real cost of the operation over the years was very reasonable and yet the asking price had seemed high. Terms and rates are significant factors.

● What will you get for your money? Take an extremely careful look at what part of the price is for good will and what part is for real property, inventory, etc. Good will is fickle. Customers devoted to one owner may not keep their devotion with a new one. I am not willing to pay much for good will.

● What's the rate of return? I paid $6,000 for the last business I bought. It's a vending route. Here's how I figured what it was worth.

The gross profit after commissions appeared to be about $5,200 a year. The time requirement was about twelve hours a month, and there were about 100 miles a month to drive. To me, that meant that I needed at least $260 a month to pay for my time and travel, maybe more. That meant the real return on my $6,000 would be cut to about $2,000 a year ($6,000 −[12 × 260]). The possibilities for expansion were fair, but I did not want to devote much time to that. I considered the expansion possibilities and the possible loss of accounts as about a trade-off. If I lost accounts, I'd find new ones but would not actively seek expansion. That meant that my $6,000 would show $2,000 a year return on invested capital, after paying me for my twelve hours a month and car expenses. A return of $2,000 a year on a $6,000 investment may sound terrific, but unlike money in a savings account, this money was invested in a rapidly depreciating asset. So the final question was how long the equipment would last. Obviously, if it was less than two years, it was a lousy venture. At $2,000 a year, I needed three years to get my investment back. Once that three years are up, my rate of return goes to infinity. I no longer have any investment, and I have a $2,000 a year income as long as it lasts. Two years are not quite up, the profits have been a little better than expected, and, while it's no get-rich-quick scheme, I think it will prove to be a very sound investment. I want to stress taking a careful look at the rate of return and insist you realize that you *must* figure in being paid for the time you use to operate your business. I've been told many times, "Buy one of these vending machines and you'll have your money back in two years. We guarantee it." I heard that from two different salesmen at the Start Your Own Business trade show. That's laughable. Buy yourself a shovel for $10, hire on as a common laborer at $2.50 an hour, and you'll have your money back in four hours, not in two years. What's more, I'll guarantee it.

The point is, if all you do is get your money back at that point, you're not even back where you started. If it takes two years "to get your money back," what about the interest you'd have earned if the money were in a savings account and, most of all, what about being paid for your time?

In evaluating any potential business, the rate of return can be based only on that share of the profit left after you pay yourself a fair and reasonable management fee for each hour you devote to the business.

Look at my vending route if you leave out the pay for my time. Gross profit: $5,200 a year. Cost: $6,000. Rate of return: almost 90 percent a year. That's a bit too good to be true. Remove a fair management fee (I'd say ten dollars an hour is minimum in today's economy, and I like to use $20 an hour), and you get the real picture. That's twelve hours a month at twenty dollars an hour for $240; 100 miles at seventeen cents a mile; and a little miscellaneous for tolls, etc. I then need to take the first $260 each month for myself before I can discuss the real rate of return. So at $260 a month for twelve months, the real profit for the year is about $2,000.

That $2,000 a year must then be viewed in terms of a 33-1/3 percent return for how many years. It's difficult to predict how many years. One question to ask is "over how many years will the IRS allow me to depreciate this asset?" If it's a new building, they are never going to allow it to be depreciated fully in three to five years. Obviously, the expected useful life of a building is much longer than that. In the case of vending equipment, three to five years is quite reasonable. A 33-1/3 percent rate of return doesn't sound so terrific if you can only expect the asset to produce that return for three years. The number of years the IRS allows for the depreciation of an asset should give a fair idea of how long you can expect it to last, and the rate of return can only be counted for that many years.

If at the end of three years, all the equipment on my vending route somehow disappears, I'll have been well paid while I managed it. I'll have gotten 33-1/3 percent return for three years, and, to me, that would mean it was a mediocre investment. You might call it a good part-time job because it paid me twenty dollars an hour. It may have given me some nice tax advantages, but the $6,000 I started with would be all I had as a return on my investment—no profit and lost interest had I had the money in a savings account.

Of course, it won't all disappear at the end of three years. Hopefully, it will go on after that, and that's why it looked like a sound investment to me. If I can own it for three years and then sell it to someone else for $6,000, it will have been a good deal. It still only means that, as an investor, I got $12,000 ($2,000 a year for three years plus $6,000 when sold) for the $6,000 I started with. That's not 100 percent profit, remember—not to me anyway. I view that as $6,000 growing to $12,000 in three years. A growth of 33-1/3 percent per year and on a risky venture is reasonable. Remember, when someone says he bought a vacant lot for $5,000 and sold it for $10,000, that's terrific if he did it in one year. Usually, the story is that he sold it ten years later. He'd have done almost as well with savings certificates. I've read a classic illustration of the same point based on the Indians selling Manhattan Island for twenty-four dollars. It pointed out that, while that seems very cheap now, if that twenty-four dollars had been put in a bank and earned interest at prevailing rates from then until now, it would have grown to more than the assessed valuation of the island today.

So, ask for tax returns to determine profits, look for growth trends, check carefully on the time it will take. Get the total picture of cost including possible financing, if any. Be certain you know how much of the cost is for real property and how much for good will, and make a detailed analysis of the real rate of return based on number of years you'll receive it and after paying yourself for your time.

Instant Business

In Chapter 3, I mentioned one disadvantage of a franchise: you may be limited in the amount of control you have. But franchises have advantages as well. They represent as close to an instant business as can be found. The parent company usually sells some kind of a package plan that almost sets the new owner into business in an instant.

They are certainly plentiful and popular. According to the Department of Commerce, 32 percent of all retail sales are made through franchises. You can probably name a dozen within a few miles of wherever you are now. My first car wash was a franchise, though I've outlasted the parent company by many years.

There's already been a great deal written about franchising. If you want a booklet full of questions to ask about a possible franchise, the SBA has one titled *Franchise Index/Profile*. Another SBA booklet lists the advantages of franchising: requires only limited experience; requires a relatively small amount of capital and provides strengthened financial and credit standing; provides a well-developed consumer image and good will with proven products and services; provides competently designed facilities, layout, displays, and fixtures; provides chain buying power; may provide training and continued assistance; and provides national or regional promotion.

The same SBA pamphlet lists these disadvantages: submission to imposed standardized operations; sharing of profits with the franchiser; lack of freedom to meet local competition; danger of contracts being slanted to the advantage of the franchiser; time consumed in preparing reports required by the franchiser; and sharing the burden of the franchiser's faults.

If you'd like a book in which the author is positive about franchising, then read the chapter on franchising in *How to Start and Manage Your Own Business* by Gardiner G. Greene or *Franchise Boom* by Harry Kursh. If you want a book that's negative on the subject, then see the section in *You, Inc.* by Peter Weaver. It also tells of other books to assist you if you're considering a franchise.

It's easy to glance at McDonald's or Midas Mufflers and get the impression that down the franchising path lies instant wealth and success. These are successful but not the sort of business you can very well do while still teaching, and the capital requirements are plenty steep.

The Franchise Directory lists over a thousand possibilities, some of which don't take much capital and can be done on a less-than-full-time basis. You can always find many represented at a business show, and you can usually find a dozen or more in the Sunday paper of any large city.

Franchises are plentiful, popular, and have advantages and disadvantages with supporters and critics. I've tried them and must say that by hard work and determination, I have made a success of a business that was a franchise and at the same time saw the franchiser go under. They can go either way but, like any business, it depends mostly on you, the owner.

So far I've covered how to finance a business, how to find the time to run one, and how to choose one you'll like (if it's possible). I've described a number of resources for finding one; where to locate; when to start; specific questions to ask about a business you're considering; and examined franchising. And yet, I suspect you may still be hesitant.

Getting Going

If you're still hesitant, let me offer two sources of inspiration: people and books.

I'd bet you know someone who has a small business and who's apparently fairly successful at it. If so, go talk to him and find out how he did it. Most American businesses are small. About one-third of the retail shops and restaurants have no employees at all. Such people can serve as a source of inspiration, and you'll find yourself saying, "If he did it, I can do it." All those millions (yes, millions) of people with their own businesses can't be that much more talented than you and I, and talking to them will convince you.

If you don't know any such people, try reading the success stories of others. If being too old is your excuse, read about Ray Kroc. He was well over fifty when he got McDonald's started. There is no such thing as too old. It's a matter of attitude, not years. If you're too busy for a business, read about Jimmy Dean's sausage company. There's a man who sure had plenty to do without getting into the sausage business, and he says he enjoys "every darn bit of the business, especially visiting meat market managers—I like to get with the guys with the bloody aprons."

Convinced you don't have enough money? Well, the brothers Trikidis had $500 when they started an art supply store in 1967. They are the same two guys whose company sold seven-and-a-half million Farrah Fawcett-Majors posters. The stories go on and on. You find them almost everywhere. Remember "pet rocks"? Now, how's that for willingness to take risks? What banker in the world could you convince to loan you money to get into the "pet rock" business? And yet it was a fantastic success because someone was willing to take the risk and make it work. Reading these success stories always gives me a lift. I guess one could read them and say, "Well, I could never do that. He had time which I don't have, he had more money than I've got, he was younger than I am when he started." I'm convinced that whatever your excuse might be, there's a full-blown success story somewhere about a person who could have used the same excuse and chose not to. Read about such people and let their successes inspire you to get going. This year alone, 500,000 new businesses will start. Be one of them.

What should you do with fear of failure, fear of losing what little money you have? Remember what that college education of yours cost? Plenty. Add to that the master's degree. No doubt the total cost was well over $1,000 dollars and probably many times that. Right? If your new business fails, you are still going to learn a great deal. Money lost in a business venture is like the cost of your college degrees: it's the price of an education. Certainly you don't think of the cost of your degrees as money lost, do you? So, if it's fear of losing some hard-earned money, then change that attitude. You don't expect to lose it, and still, if you do, focus on what you've learned.

That's fine, you say, but I don't have much money and if I lost everything now, my family would suffer. Start small, but *get going*. First, start small.

H. S. Kahm has written a book, *101 Businesses You Can Start and Run with Less than $1,000*. It's my kind of book. There are only eight introductory pages and over 200 pages listing the specific 101 businesses, all the way from caramel corn to karate, from wake-up service to rent-a-girl. There are three brief, clear sections on each business. The first tells you what the business is, the second tells how to get started, and the third tells how much you can make. With 101 choices, aren't you apt to find one or two that, with willingness to work and perseverance, could be a success? Remember, these can be started with $1,000 or less, and, while I find some of the suggestions in the book might be tough going with only $1,000, there are many where it's clear to me you can actually get going on far less than $1,000. So try one for the fun, excitement, and the education you'll get. It also can mean money well spent regardless of any eventual profit. Think of it as a personal declaration of independence and take the risk. Try being your own boss—you'll like it. The cost is far less than those degrees. It's the price of an education.

Now, with 101 choices for a small start, here's a neat trick to get you going. As soon as you have picked one, here's what Peter Weaver in his book, *You, Inc.*, says to do. It brought with it good feelings of progress, pride, and independence that I had vaguely experienced each time I'd done it, but not until I read Weaver's book, had those feelings been so precisely clear as to cause.

Name the business and open a checking account. Weaver says, ".... think of some business name that fits your personality or the idea you want to develop." In Chapter 3, I told of my painting business. We were not just painters. Printed on my checks was "The Painting Teachers." We had an identity, and those printed checks were useful when I needed to get contractors' prices at paint stores where I was unknown. Notice we were not just "Painting Teachers" but "The Painting Teachers," as if there were no others. Each time I used those checks, I was reminded of who I was, and those who received them saw who we were. I suspect it produced some extra business. Many people may have heard that a few teachers paint in the summertime. Out of fond memories for some teacher, a belief they might be cheaper, or a desire to do business with responsible people, many folks were willing to hire teachers to paint. But how could they find us? At some point, people who are going to have their houses painted will probably go to a paint store. To all the stores where we bought paint and supplies, we were "The Painting Teachers." We had the checks to prove it, so people found out about us.

Weaver has more to say about checking accounts as a

means to get going.

"So what's all the fuss about opening a checking account with your new venture's name? Because it's probably the first time you've actually committed some money to your cause, and the name of your game is right down on those checks in bold print where everybody can see it. It gives much-needed importance to your cause. When you buy supplies or pay for legitimate business expenses, those you're dealing with can see you have some kind of organization. You're not just working on an out-of-pocket lark.

"Even more important, your own checkbook is a real focus point for your business. There it is. You've taken the first big step. It serves as a daily reminder. That little bank account jogs your conscience and demands to be fed."

It seems to me the essence of the psychology of opening the checking account can be applied in other ways. The notion of committing some of your money to the project seems to be the critical part. Once you have made the initial investment, you're on your way. Business cards and stationery would reinforce the situation and give that same feeling of seeing the company name in print.

To be really committed, I like to place an order for something more directly used in making a profit. From the moment I order a new piece of equipment, I'm thinking about how soon it will start paying for itself. I recently ordered some new vending machines for paper towels and whitewall cleaner to be sold at car washes. Once ordered and delivered, I lost no time getting them installed because I wanted to see them start paying for themselves, and I was curious to see if people would pay a quarter for a paper towel to dry their car. (They will.) In starting any business, spending your money for the initial inventory to sell a product, or for the lawn mowers if you're going to cut grass, or the ladders and brushes if you're going to paint houses, will put you in a position where the next move is obvious. Sell the inventory, cut the lawns, paint the houses. From then on, the profits will be the motivation to keep going.

If you want a business you can operate in your home read *Profits at Your Doorstep*. It's a Barnes and Noble paperback by Judith Weber and Karol White. It seemed to me to be aimed a bit at women who are housewives and yet has sections on how to sell what you produce, on mail order, on the characteristics of business tycoons and even an aptitude test to supposedly help determine if you'd be good at a business in your home and if so which kind would be best. The book is subtitled *A Complete Guide to Setting Up A Successful Business in Your Home*.

If you get started (and I hope you're thinking seriously about it), then the next chapter will provide some thoughts on how to keep your small business smooth-running and profitable.

6

Suggestions to Insure Successful Operation

Most businesses in America are small businesses. Depending on which definition of "small" one chooses, 90 percent of American businesses are labeled small. And many people are making a small business operate profitably. There are also quite a few failures. For new businesses, the failure rate is staggering. One-third fail in the first year, half in the first two years, and two-thirds are gone before their fifth birthday. Here are some common causes of failure, along with some suggestions to insure successful operation.

According to Dun and Bradstreet's Business Failure Record, less than 1 percent fail due to fraud, less than 1 percent due to neglect, and less than 1 percent due to disaster. It's poor management that accounts for over 90 percent of the failures, and by poor management, Dun and Bradstreet mean lack of experience or incompetence resulting in inadequate sales, inability to be competitive, heavy operating expenses, difficulty with accounts receivable or inventory, or excessive fixed assets. Almost half of the failures are at the retail level, with construction second and manufacturing

105

third. The rate of failure has been in general decline since about 1961 but had been steadily increasing from 1945 to 1961. So the statistics on failure make the field look a little risky, and there's no denying you're going to be taking a risk although these Dun and Bradstreet figures seem to me to make it sound more risky than I've experienced it to be

Those Fancy Frills

My first suggestions concern frills. There are many businesses that appear to me to waste unbelievable sums (at least to a teacher) on unnecessary frills. I know this may be good business in some cases, but I also know it must be seriously questionable in others. Keep a sharp eye for what is necessary versus what looks good.

Some used equipment is give-away cheap. My adding machine cost five dollars. It may look a bit old and be a bit large by today's standards, but its answers are as correct as any. My typewriter, an IBM Executive, cost fifty dollars with a trade-in. I believe it was over $700 when new. It may not have all the latest features, but it prints a letter each time I strike a key. Automobiles can be very elaborate frills. (Reread the section about cars in Chapter 4.) I guess admonitions about waste are an age-old practice, but when some small business spends more on office furniture and decorations than an average teacher makes in a year, then it's time to be cautious.

Tools of the Trade

Good tools are not frills. Whatever the business, there will be tools of the trade, sometimes in the very literal meaning of tools, and sometimes not.

In the car wash business (like any other), there are some special situations. Some you can get through with patience and a pair of pliers but others do call for special tools. Any job attempted with poor or unsuitable tools is sure to end in frustration. Absence of proper tools is apt to lead to delayed maintenance and postponed repairs and improvements. For work to be enjoyable, the tools need to be designed for the job, not ones that might do. I could change my spark plugs with a crescent wrench. It would be a knuckle-buster, plug-buster, and temper-loser, but it's possible. With the correct socket set, it's quick, safe, and enjoyable. Buy the tools you need, and pay to acquire the skills you need. Anything that saves time and frustration is not a frill.

The tools of your business may not be the kind that go in a tool box. My notion of tool goes beyond the set I always have in the back of my station wagon. Anything that will motivate you to work, get you looking forward to a task in your business, is a worthwhile tool, even if only indirectly used to get a job done.

As a teacher, you face the task of motivating students

on a daily basis. You know it takes considerable ingenuity to figure out what will motivate the students, and you know that what works on some will not work on others. So ask yourself what motivates you. Is there a "tool" which will maximize your motivation for working? If there is, it is as important to you as the proper socket wrench to the man who's changing spark plugs. When it came to writing this book, a trip to the office supply store gave me some "tools" which motivated me. As a teacher, of course, I had pens, paper, etc.—all one needs to write. Somehow, buying all new tablets, new files, new pens, gave me some added incentive to work at it. I've been back a second time already and also added some shelving to my office. All these things were unessential to the task at hand, and yet to me, they have been motivational "tools." Figure out what yours are, and buy them.

Pricing

To raise prices or not to raise prices, that is the question. Each time we have considered raising car wash prices, we have been afraid it might cost us customers in the long run, i.e., the net result might be less profit instead of more. Usually, we have waited until there was a noticeable drop in profits due to increased costs. Dropping profits tend to make one postpone improvements, reduce repairs to minimum, and continue to use equipment that should have been updated or replaced. Of course, once the profit squeeze is tight enough, it becomes obvious that prices have to be raised.

No customer of any business likes to see prices go up. Yet people living with the inflation rates that we have had the last few years are expecting them to increase. Here we were, afraid to raise prices, and all the time our customers were expecting them to go up. Maintaining quality is more important than the price you must charge to make a profit. As long as your prices are somewhat competitive, keep raising them as your costs increase. It's the American way, and Americans are expecting it.

Keeping Abreast

Keep abreast of the industry you're in. Subscribe to the trade papers for your industry. These will tell you what's new and what is going on with folks in similar situations.

In the coin-operated car wash industry, much of the original equipment was made from components that were designed for use in laundromats. It was generally ill-suited to outdoor applications like ours. Before I subscribed to the trade journals, I designed and had fabricated some better equipment. It solved the problem it was supposed to, and it was very expensive. When I later started reading the trade papers, I found out that equipment similar to my design was available and being produced on a much larger scale. I had had the fun of designing my own, but it was time-consuming and expensive. Mass-produced equipment is apt to be cheaper and more quickly available, and you'll find out about it in industry trade papers.

Purchasing

In almost every business, there's purchasing to be done. Anything you purchase for your business from a truck to a box of paper clips is a legitimate expense of doing business, so keep track (pay with a company check) of these for tax purposes.

The rule of good purchasing is the same for business as it is for weekly groceries. There are multiple sources of supply competing with one another, and the purchaser selects the best buy from the many sources available. In business, I like to be sure I have multiple sources of supply. Not only is it good for them to compete with one another for my purchases, but on occasion, if my usual supplier is out of stock, I have alternate sources to turn to.

I was recently in the market for coin-operated vacuum cleaners. These items were available from four local distributors that I knew of, and I had purchased them from one of these local firms on two previous occasions. I decided to search for other sources and not limit my search to the local area.

I took one of the trade papers for the industry and

began calling all over the country. I had drawn a list of questions to ask each. Were they manufacturers or distributors? I asked technical questions about product quality, price, and availability. The first manufacturer would not sell to me; I had to buy through his local distributor. Most of the out-of-town distributors were quoting about the same price I could get locally. On the ninth call, I hit a manufacturer who would sell to me. Before the end of our conversation, I discovered he made the vacuums for four of the distributors I had talked to. He said this was done under a private label arrangement, and the same machines were available directly to me if I wanted them. Within a week, I had four new coin-operated vacuum cleaners and paid less than I would have for two from the local distributor selling the same machines under a private label. Mine are a different color and have a different label but otherwise are the same—except, of course, for the cost.

More and more I'm finding out that I can eliminate middlemen. Some manufacturers in our industry will sell direct or through distributors. Direct is cheaper.

I've also found that many places which claim to be wholesale only will sell to anyone in business, and retailers will give discounts to other businesses. The local hardware store gives me 10 percent off on all purchases because I have a business account there. I buy light bulbs at an electrical supply house that's "wholesale only." They know my money spends just like the electrician's who's standing at the counter beside me. Same for plumbing supplies, motors, and so on. Once in a while, I get asked who I'm "with," but purchasing with a company check seems to satisfy them.

Purchasing is an important part of owning any business. The closer you get to the original manufacturer, the cheaper the goods are apt to be. Don't think you're too small. All businesses want to sell their products, and, wholesale or retail, your money is as good as anyone else's.

Business Relationships

Cultivate relationships with other owners of similar businesses and with the suppliers and service people for your industry. These people can be a great resource. The owners face and solve the same problems that you do.

Over the years, I have maintained periodic contact with a lady who started a coin-operated car wash just a few weeks before we opened our first one. I sort of make biannual offers to buy hers from her, but she knows the joy of owning a small business herself and has steadfastly declined my offers. On the occasion of my last call, after we had compared profits and talked of ways to improve business, I once again raised the possibility of my buying her out. No, she didn't want to sell but if I wanted another one, she had heard from a service man she had doing some repair work that there was one for sale. It was an installation I was familiar with and if the price she'd heard was right, it was a steal. It was. We now own it but the purchase involved a weird situation.

The asking price was $10,000, but it was that low because the owner needed immediate cash. In addition, he had a buyer who had purchased it, changed his mind, and backed out of the deal. We bought it and allowed thirty days to get the paper work done before we were to take over. The owner was a man who'd been in the business as long as I had, and I had been remotely acquainted with him since we both started.

About two weeks before take-over, he called to say he had received a definite cash offer of $15,000. He wasn't asking to get out of our agreement, but he wanted to let me know he was tempted. Now, that made for an interesting situation.

In business, a deal is a deal—or so it's supposed to be. The money had not yet changed hands and the choices seemed to be to insist on going ahead with original deal, agree to match the new offer, or try for a compromise somewhere between the two, the closer to the original the better.

Insisting on the original deal might work and yet, no money had changed hands and if it came to a court battle, there would be delays and legal expenses and always the chance we'd lose. In addition, the original price was so low that to pay more would be unpleasant but still leave us with an excellent investment. We went for the compromise and, while it seems a bit strange to wind up paying $12,000 when the asking price was $10,000, it was worth the $12,000 and then some. The point is that keeping in contact with other owners put me in touch with an opportunity that's not only turning out to be a sound investment but had a very memorable twist to it as well.

The suppliers and service people see a wide variety of owners in the industry. It's true they are in business to get you to buy from them, but a genuinely friendly relationship is apt to prompt them to give you the best information that they have as well as emergency service when you need it.

Smooth-running Partnerships

I've indicated in an earlier section my preference for partnerships. But how do you choose good partners and keep the partnership running smoothly?

In choosing partners, ask yourself what you need from a partner. Is he going to contribute needed capital? Is it his time you need to help run the business, or does he have knowledge or skills that you don't have? Some or all of these assets should be present in the partner you choose.

I doubt if two Irish, Catholic, Democrat, high school math teachers who collect old cars for a hobby would make ideal partners. Diversification of talent, time, and interest are very apt to be missing. In choosing a partner, his capital, time, and knowledge are the assets, but beyond this, you need someone who's available when you're not, whose business background is somewhat different from a teacher's, and, hopefully, someone who's good at the things you're not and likes to be responsible for those aspects of business for which you don't like to be responsible. If both of you can't stand to keep books, you can always figure on hiring a bookkeeping service, but it's nice if there is sufficient diversification of talent and interest, likes and dislikes, to minimize the number of outsiders your business will need.

Of course, an ability to get along with one another is critical. A partner with lots of time to devote to the business but with whom you can't get along is not usually much of an asset to you. The fact that you have previously gotten along well socially may not guarantee you'll get along well in business. Money can bend a friendly relationship all out of shape. Just how good a working relationship you'll have is difficult to predict. Some of mine have been good and some not so good. I can tell you that having more than two people in a partnership has been more difficult for me to work with than a single partner. Since I know it's difficult to predict a successful partnership, the upcoming section on smooth-running partnerships will include what to do when and if it comes to a split up.

There are some very real risks when dealing with

partners. The danger is that one partner will perceive himself as doing more than his share of the work while receiving his usual share of the profit. A second risk is that partners will disagree on what is to be done or on how to do it. Here are my suggestions to minimize such risks:

1. Divide the responsibilities as clearly and as evenly as possible, and, once divided, leave one another alone.

2. If it seems more logical for one man to do a greater share of the work, then he should receive a greater share of the profit. How to decide what's fair? Have one partner name a dollar figure or a percent of the profit at which he will be willing to do the work or have his partner do it. The other partner then has the option of doing the work or letting his partner do it for the increased pay.

3. Many disagreements about what should be done (expand, don't expand) are based not so much on what it will cost or produce in profit but on who will do the work of making the changes. The only sure way to find out if a change will increase profits is to try it. The risk isn't the problem; getting the work done is. If you favor the change, then ask your partner, "are you willing to go along with this if I do the work?" Then, if and when it has increased profits, you can use suggestion number two to continue with it.

4. Agree in the beginning to resolve differences that are not resolvable otherwise by the toss of a coin. It's quick, simple, and saves the agony of those long and repetitious arguments.
5. If it comes to a split-up, and it happened to me and many others, then one partner names the price and terms at which he will sell his share (assuming each is a 50 percent share) or buy out his partner.
6. No matter which partner keeps the books, both must have full access to them, and it must be an access that does not make the keeper of the books feel that his trust is being questioned.

Time Well Spent and Goals Well Set

In any business, how the owner spends his time is important. Ownership is a responsibility-laden role. On the one hand, you should be willing to tackle any task necessary to the success of your adventure, and on the other hand, not too much of your time should be spent doing things that require little talent or skill. Those can be done by others. I don't mind picking up trash and papers at the car washes when I'm there and walking over them anyway. But that's a simple enough (though very necessary) task that I would not be wise to spend much of my time doing.

Keep track of how you spend your business hours. If they're not largely devoted to ownership types of responsibilities, then delegate those to others, preferably through contractual arrangements. Owners should spend time on making the business more profitable.

Besides analyzing how much time you spend on ownership responsibilities, keep track of what tasks you find most frustrating. Frustrating tasks are very apt to be neglected or at least postponed, and that can be bad for business. Once the frustrating ones are identified, then see about not having to do them. If you're in a partnership, it could well be that those tasks you find frustrating, your partner will find enjoyable (diversification of interest). If both partners find the task frustrating or if there is no partner, then get someone else to do them. Do the same in teaching. My partner who's a physics teacher dislikes grading lab reports. He pays a fellow physics teacher to grade them for him and pays his wife to keep track of homework scores in a business math course he teaches. To force oneself to do tasks that one knows to be frustrating is sometimes necessary but usually not healthy. It's money well spent (in business or teaching) to have them done for you if possible.

It took lots of planning and goal-setting to become a teacher. You have to set goals for your students (or get them to set them) in whatever course you teach, and you certainly have to plan your classes for each day and each semester. So it is in business, too. Those same goal-setting procedures and planning techniques that you use in teaching will work in business. In fact, it seems easier to me to set goals and make plans that lead to a profit than to get students to appreciate, understand, and perhaps even develop a proof for Pythagoras's theorem.

So, watch the frills; buy necessary tools and motivational "tools"; when costs go up, raise your prices; keep abreast of your industry; purchase wisely; cultivate useful relationships; choose partners carefully; keep the partnership running smoothly; spend your time mostly on ownership responsibilities; and set goals and make plans just like you do in teaching.

7

And Besides the $30,000 a Year

Interested in Money?

Besides making money and thus making a living while teaching full time, I feel my business experience has made me a better teacher. As a teacher, you no doubt know that many students are not interested in some subjects. Perhaps one of the greatest challenges in teaching is to get the students interested, and it's not easy to do. I'm not even sure it's possible. I'm afraid that some of those subjects are not very interesting.

I have a theory that interest on the part of some students is developed like this. First they find their teacher interesting, then they see that their teacher is interested in the subject. The student then becomes willing to explore the subject because the teacher he finds interesting is interested in the subject. My students seem fascinated by how I make money (who's not interested in money?). Once interested in me and how I make money, I then am an odds-on favorite to get them interested in academic things. I guess that's both vain and oversimplified—but it works.

The Joys—but I Only Expected $10

If you're teaching in one of those schools where the median income of most students' families is well above teachers' pay, you may have encountered an attitude on the part of some of the students that implies you can't really have much talent or you wouldn't be teaching. If you could make more money doing other things, you would, but you can't, so you teach. (Sound familiar?) I believe it's an attitude that the students pick up from their parents. While it's certainly not the attitude of all students or all parents, I have taught in at least one school where I perceived that attitude as widespread. It is an attitude of disrespect. It judges people by how much money they have, and it's certainly not an attitude I like to see in our youth. At one time, I felt defensive about it. Now it's an attitude I can deal with comfortably. My above-average income bought me (indirectly) that comfort. I now welcome the chance to discuss money with students, to attempt to reshape their attitudes so that they will not judge people by how much money they make. I welcome the chance to tell them what joys money can produce. And I'm going to tell you, though it may well sound corny.

To me, the biggest joy is having enough money to be able to give it away. I've gotten lots of unbelievable looks turned into warm smiles when I've handed someone fifty or a hundred dollars. I feel great when I give people who are asking for contributions ten times the amount they ever expect to get from a teacher. I believe that hearing of that joy may have motivated a student or two to rethink their values.

Along with making money and becoming a better teacher (I think), there have been personal benefits as well as strains. I'll mention the benefits to encourage you to try it and the strains and pains so that you can try to avoid them.

There's nothing like financial success to build confidence. I no longer have the doubts I once had about my ability to make money. Each small success gives the courage and confidence needed to try another business. And each successful business brings more confidence. Despite some trying moments and some failures, I *can* teach and make a living at the same time.

Efficient but Critical

When my associates and I had our merit pay proposal passed, it did more for me than raise my salary. I worked many hours and did a lot of pushing, persuading, and convincing. I'm glad I did it. In the process, I began to question my efficiency. Would an equal amount of time and energy spent elsewhere produce more results for me? I didn't know, but I knew how to find out. I had a hunch there would never be good money in education, that what seemed like enormous raises to teachers were commonplace to many businessmen. The top salaries in teaching were not even comparable to the upper salaries in business. So I went after the answer. Would the time and energy produce more for me in business? I can tell you for sure, the answer is yes. Since being in both business and teaching, I've learned a lot about efficiency, about managing time, spending time wisely.

In a way, that efficiency accounts for one of the strains. I have a hunch that some of my fellow teachers feel that I am critical of them. But it's no hunch when it comes to administrators. I *am* critical of them.

The analogies between teaching (not administration) and business can be bad. I think most are. The only one I like is accountability. In business, we go by results— profits or losses. In education, students should be accountable for what's to be learned. If they have not met what you judge to be minimum standards, then their grade should be F. Teachers cannot guarantee that students will learn; some are simply unwilling to learn. What we should guarantee is that the grades they receive reflect what they know. It is absolutely unthinkable to graduate a student from grade school who can't read. Where's the liar who gave him a passing grade? I say round up all those liars and drum them out of the teaching corps. See why my peers think I'm critical?

Please notice that I said most analogies between teaching and business (except accountability) are bad. Now, when it comes to administering education (which is not teaching, no way is it teaching), then most of the analogies are on target. In business, professional people have phones, offices, secretaries, etc. Who has those sort of things in your school? You're damn right: *they* do and you do not. (See why the administrators think I'm critical?)

When Marc Murdock and I found a storeroom at our high school and began using it as an office, that was unusual. When we asked that a phone be installed, we got that "you don't know your place" look. We had one put in at our own expense, and believe it or not, they started paying the bill after three months. It's still got a long, long way to go. Fights with administrators are often silly by business standards. In our building, there must be a dozen electric typewriters. The administrators have them, the secretaries have them. But there is not a single electric typewriter available to teachers (to say nothing of a secretary to type for us). We have three manual typewriters for a faculty of over 40. The list could go on and on, and you, no doubt, could supply a long one of your own.

I've found that administrators don't like to have me apply those business analogies and I've slowed down a lot. It's too much strain, too inefficient in terms of gains—and administrators resent it. So, a word of caution. Teachers and administrators (like all folks) don't take too fondly to criticism. Most are good people trying to do their best in difficult circumstances. Learning is not as simple as profit and loss. Go easy on your associates, use tact and much patience, and bite your tongue once in a while. Still, just for the fun of it,

and with a big smile on your face, go ask your principal
if you can use his office, his fancy desk, his phone, and
his secretary for just one afternoon.

Cocktails, Status, Families, and Temptations

Ever been to one of those cocktail parties where you
meet strangers? Where one of the first questions is
"What do you do?" The type of party where doctors
somehow manage to make it known in the first two
sentences of conversation that they are DOCTORS. And
have you ever experienced just a moment's hesitancy at
saying I'm a teacher? I used to. It's that old game of
oneupmanship. I can't always resist playing and now
it's far more fun than it used to be. "I own an interest in a
car wash," etc., etc., etc. I'll give them two paragraphs
about my business and finish off with "I also teach math
full time, you know, just to have something to do."

Of course, the point is not to win at oneupmanship.
That, incidentally, is best won by lying. I'll tell them I'm
in real estate, aviation, and shipping (you know, boats).
After all, I do own a house, one of my partners is taking
flying lessons, and one owns a speed boat. No, the point
is that teachers, because of the status (pay) that
American society now places on them, are a somewhat
self-pitying and perhaps downtrodden lot. Some have
always managed to avoid those sorts of feelings and be
comfortable in knowing or believing that teaching is a
noble profession. To me, many of us are not

comfortable with where society places us. I wasn't and business success has changed that. My income places me well into the top 10 percent of all working people. That means I'm a nine-to-one favorite to actually be one-up on those clowns I meet at cocktail parties. More importantly, though, most of my time and energy are still devoted to that noble endeavor of seeing to it that the young learn. It feels good.

Does the dual role put a strain on family life? I'm afraid it does, especially in the beginning when it was more of a struggle, and each time I start a new venture. I've always been aware of my responsibilities to my wife and children. I may have seen myself too much as a provider and not enough as a husband and father. Even with good efficiency, it's easy to neglect them at times, and I have. So another word of caution: start young, before you marry or before you have children. If it's too late for that, by all means, start anyway, but be careful. I've worked my last full-time summer. Now, in the summers, I do about fifteen hours a week of business or a little more, but I probably could have started doing that years ago. It took a serious illness to bring me to the realization that from now on, summers will have a lot more family time.

A word of warning: there will always be a temptation to give up teaching. Once you see that the business world is not all that rough, that you're about as successful as many businessmen and more successful than some, and that making money is no more difficult than teaching, you may start asking yourself "Why not quit teaching, devote full time to my business, and then make the really big money?" Has greed at last reared its ugly head? Is your need for achievement that strong, or do you like being your own boss that well? Whatever your reason, it's been a very real temptation, perhaps strongest on those days when it seems that not one student has learned anything, and, for some reason I can't quite identify, half of the students come to class (seemingly at the time) for the sole purpose of seeing if they can aggravate me. Ever had one of those days? Those are the days when the temptation to go for the really big money is strong (greed and the need of achievement?). For me, those days are few and far between. If for you, though, such days are many and frequent, I'd say go. For I suspect you'll find the same kind of days in full-time business. But if you're having them frequently in teaching, I've got a strong hunch the students will be better off with you in the business world full time. If and when those kind of days become frequent for me, I hope I'll be aware of it and realize it's time to move on.

Even with few such days, I still feel the urge now and then. I even try to rationalize it by saying go on, make a fortune, you'll use it wisely, you can set up an educational foundation, or start a school of your own. *Maybe!*

With the greed and the need for achievement is also the fear that as a teacher and businessman I'm a success, but that as a full-time businessman I'd be a flop. I'm quite sure that doubling my teaching income and making really big money are in two different leagues. It may be a situation where I'm pushing the limit of what I could do in the business field. Who knows? Have I risen to my level of incompetence already?

I am convinced that bigger is not always better. I think there have been lots of small businesses where the owner was doing well and enjoying doing what he was doing. The notion to expand comes along, and in a few short years, the man who used to have fun repairing bicycles in his one-man shop finds himself spending most of his time as an administrator supervising a staff of twenty at six different locations. Instead of having a spoke wrench in his hand and a wheel on his workbench, he has a pen in his hand and piles of paper on his desk. He may be making more money, but he's no longer doing what he really liked to do. The boys who used to look over his workbench and speak to him of aligning wheels have been replaced by salesmen who look over his desk and speak to him of making deals. His bank account tells him he's more successful, but his indigestion tells him he's not.

Certainly not all small businesses that have grown to big ones have produced owners with indigestion. Some were dreaming of pens and desks while working with the wrenches at the workbench. The point is to be doing what you want to do and what you enjoy. If making your small part-time business into a large full-time one is what you would like to do and enjoy doing, that's fine. Still, recall before you do so that it was started so you could make a living and teach at the same time and ask yourself how you can own and manage a large full-time business and teach, too. You may be asking for indigestion!

The temptation to quit teaching and go for really big money may not be the dangerous one. I've felt it and am still teaching. Yet my business holdings are larger than ever and growing. Just talking about another one produces frowns from my wife. New business ventures are apt to be quite demanding on your time in their first few months of operation, and since teaching comes first, the additional time may be taken from your family or from the hours you sleep or both. I'd sure like to find a way to cut my need for sleep in half because I've seen some businesses that look very interesting and I fantasize about my next book (after another 20 years of teaching) about how to make a million while teaching full time.

The serious point is that success in business has not only given me the confidence and money I needed, it has tempted me to try more and different businesses. But there's a limit to how many of those can be done without compromising the quality of your teaching or the responsibilities to your family. Each time I start a new one, I try to shift one of the existing ones to a contractual management situation whereby someone has a contract to run the business. I retain ownership and the buck still stops in my office and that's the buck that's passed to me when there are serious problems, as well as the bucks of profit. These contractual arrangements have given me more time to sleep, but they don't have my wife frowning any less when there's talk of a new venture.

If you are a good teacher and enjoy teaching, I hope you'll stay. However, if you leave, make that fortune, and retire, I hope you teach and use the fortune instead of this book to make a living as a teacher. Otherwise, you may be spending the fortune looking for cures for indigestion.

So, besides the money, you'll become a better, more interesting, and more efficient teacher. I think you'll be more confident and more comfortable with being a teacher. Be aware of the temptations that lead to indigestion.

And instead of arguing with administrators for an electric typewriter, buy yourself one and spend the time you saved with your wife and family.

8

Teaching and Education

Because this book is titled *How to Teach School and Make a Living at the Same Time,* the focus has been on how to make a living while teaching. Yet, the title contains "how to teach" and so I'm including a few pages that focus on six facets of teaching or education: motivation, accountability for students, accountability for teachers, role of administrators, coaches and sports, and my three favorite books. If you're only interested in the money part, I'll save you some time by telling you to skip this chapter.

I offer no magic formula on the best way to teach. I'm not reporting on educational research and I'm not going to cite evidence from statistical studies. By no means am I the best teacher in the area—some at my school are better. I have more experience than some and less than others, more training than some and less than others. So, these are my opinions about teaching. For whatever they are worth, I own them.

Motivation

The educational literature is filled with articles about motivation. The great failure of education is often cited as the failure to motivate students. Educational difficulties would disappear if only the students received proper motivation from their teachers. Now, I can't be against motivation and I'm not. Still, as strongly as I believe in it, I feel a few comments are necessary to keep it in proper perspective.

From some of the comments I've heard about motivation, a teacher could be led to believe he could have all his students flying around the room if only he motivated them properly. What crap.

I view the doorway to motivation as one that is locked from the inside. I can knock on the door, but if the student refuses entry, that's his problem. I can knock in different ways for different students and I'll knock repeatedly, but I can accept being denied entry. It overstates my case to say it, but I will: you can't motivate a stone.

I'm afraid a good bit of what I read about motivation is aimed at hooking a teacher's guilt. I dislike that. I'll not feel guilty when my repeated and varied knocks don't gain me entry. The student's side of learning calls for some intellectual curiosity. Given zero intellectual curiosity, motivation is not apt to compensate for it. So, do everything you can in every way you can to motivate students, and then be satisfied with that.

Accountability for Students

At the other end of motivation is the "make them do

the work or else" sort of thinking. In my early days of teaching, I did a lot of that, and I still see a lot of it going on today.

Students are assigned work and if it isn't done, they are verbally lacerated or punished. Fear of reprisals and intimidation are the tools of such teaching. "I'll make your life so miserable, you'll never skip doing one of my assignments again" is how the approach goes. Confrontation in front of the class is the common technique.

That's out in my classes. I assign daily work and tell the students it's assigned to help them learn math. The trouble is, there is not a "best way" to learn math. Some learn it best by watching the teacher do examples, some by reading the book, and some by working with someone else. There are many ways to learn. The goal is for the student to learn to be responsible for his own learning. As long as he learns math, how he learns it is secondary.

The student is accountable for learning, not for doing assignments. As long as he can demonstrate his knowledge of math on achievement tests, I'm satisfied. If he can't pass the exams, his grade should be F. I believe in giving students an opportunity to fail! I do not believe in forcing them to do assignments. If forced, they're likely to learn more about how to copy effectively than about math. Failure is a part of life. Experience with failure is not evil. We learn from failure. A student should constantly be developing responsibility for himself. Self-responsibility is not learned by being intimidated into doing assignments. It is learned by being given increasing amounts of self-responsibility and by analyzing the failures, if any, as they occur. The greatest sort of disservice occurs when a student has not learned and yet is given passing grades anyway. That's corrupt. Each year, I ask students, "Did you really learn any math last year?" Most did; some did not. Then I ask about their grades. There are always too many whose grades seem to indicate they know their math, and yet they know full well they don't.

The older they are, the more self-responsibility they should be developing. Certainly by the time they're in senior high school, they should no longer be forced to do work. They should be free to choose, and if they choose not to learn, they should be given the opportunity, through accountability, to experience failure.

Accountability for Teachers

As I said in the first chapter, I'd like to see state board exams in subject matter areas as a prerequisite to getting a teaching license.

Once you're in the classroom, accountability should go on. I think I know two ways to keep teachers accountable, and one way which I believe is seriously questionable.

First, the questionable one: the classroom visit by the supervisor or principal. They're fine but unless he's going to visit for weeks at a time, the atmosphere in the classroom is apt to be quite different with the principal present than with him absent.

I'm a trifle ashamed to admit it, but here's what I once did so a class and I would look good on these visiting days. A certain student had a number memorized. He knew that if I called on him on visitor's day, his number would be the answer to whatever question I asked. No matter how complicated an equation I'd toss out, if he was called upon to answer, his number would be the one that worked. I simply rigged the questions that way. He'd pause for a few seconds, look as if he were calculating feverishly, and out would pop the right answer. We always looked good to visitors.

Another teacher I knew would always back up to material he was sure the students knew whenever a visitor was present. They probably looked as good as we did.

I've seldom found such visits to be much help, and usually they are promised in far greater numbers than ever actually take place. I've heard of schools where they are frequent but, in my twenty years, I've had less than a dozen. I don't think principals like making them and I've never known one to visit so frequently that his presence went unnoticed.

Now to the two ways that I believe do work. I've

experienced both of these and I like them.

In the first school where I taught algebra, we were given a syllabus for the course and a model final exam, and were told that at the end of the year, all algebra students would be given such an exam by the administration. Each class was rated for math aptitude. When the test results of the final exam were in, some pretty obvious conclusions would surface. If your class had significantly higher average scores on the achievement exam given by administration than a class of equal aptitude, you looked good. If you had the group with the best average math aptitude in the class and the group did not have the highest average score on the achievement test, you didn't look so good. Your evaluation depended on the performance-aptitude ratio of your group. It kept us working pretty hard and let the loafers know they were not getting the job done as well as the man down the hall.

In any fairly large high school where there are multiple sections of certain basic courses, an achievement exam based on the syllabus for the course will give some interesting information about the students and about the teachers.

The second method of accountability is student evaluation. I like it. I had a principal who once kept all the students in homeroom and gave them teacher evaluation forms for each of their teachers. The form was divided into nineteen topics, each topic with a rating scale from one to ten.

Homeroom that morning lasted over an hour. Each homeroom teacher collected all the forms and sent them to the office. Each teacher's forms were put together and an average score for him was obtained on each of the nineteen topics. Each teacher was then given the median score for all the staff and his own scores so he could see how he rated.

Finally, each teacher's average in each of the nineteen categories was totaled. With a total score on each teacher, all the teachers could then be ranked from best to worst—and they were.

The evaluation was not popular with the teachers. It could be legitimately questioned on several grounds. I heard it disclaimed, denied, and damned. It was very threatening to a lot of teachers. Some said the students had no right to evaluate them and that a low rating from the students is what a "good" teacher should get.

I had no way of finding out all the scores (damn it), but I asked a few friends and we shared our scores. It went too far to say the survey could rank the teachers first, second, third, fourth, etc. That abused the data a bit. Still, I'm confident the poorer teachers did receive lower ratings than the better ones, and those people who ranked near the top were some of the best teachers with whom I've ever been associated.

Student evaluation has a place in teacher accountability and, while such data could be misused, I never let a year go by that I don't ask the students to fill out such a form about me, and any administrator who wants them to do one for him is welcome to it.

So for teacher accountability, I believe I have three pieces of the puzzle: state board exams in subject matter, performance-aptitude ratios of their students, and student evaluations.

What do we do with these data? If the data are very strong, the pay should go way up. If the data are weak, it's time to move on. I mentioned merit pay in Chapter 1. I know it's about as popular as a fly in the punch bowl, but I'm for it. Without evaluation and reward, we're apt to guarantee mediocrity.

The Role of Administrators

In my ideal model of a school, the teachers are there to serve the students, to assist them in learning, even inspire them to learn, facilitate their learning. There's more to it than that, but allowing for a bit of oversimplification, that's it.

What are the administrators there for? They are there to serve the teachers, to assist them in teaching, even inspire them to teach, facilitate their teaching. There's more to it than that, but allowing for a little over-simplification, that's it.

I've known some teachers who fit that ideal model pretty well. Most teachers I know at least accept the essence of it as the ideal of what teaching is all about.

Now, when it comes to administrators, I'm afraid it's another story. Many will accept the ideal somewhere in their list of priorities, but many wouldn't. I've now served students under nine or ten different principals. Their job is not easy and their hours are long. They are usually former teachers who know what it's like to be in the classroom. But once they become principals or assistant principals, they seem to have had brain transplants.

I judge them by the way they spend their time. Usually a good portion of it is devoted to public relations. I can't fight good PR. Often another large portion is devoted to seeing students. Who could criticize them for that? The last third of their time goes to paperwork—the endless string of forms to be filled out and questionnaires to be answered. Now, that leaves very little time to directly serve the faculty. Granted, these aforementioned duties serve the faculty indirectly. I accept that, but I recall teaching under one man where a student or a parent had a much easier time getting to see him than a member of his own faculty.

Almost all the administrators under whom I've served were good at sending memos. These usually tell the teacher how he can be of service to administration. Proctor this bathroom, get grades in by this date, use this form to report absences but that one to report tardies and the green one to report nude students with missing nostrils who are riding their motorcycles in the elevator shafts.

I have not received many memos asking how they could serve me better; very few asking for details on how they could facilitate my teaching. And if I'd ever received a memo that inspired me to teach better, I'd surely have framed it in gold.

I've come to the conclusion that even principals who accept my ideal model have little chance to do much about it. If they were more autonomous, more decisive, and better time managers, they might be able to devote more effort toward it and, yet, in many cases, they are trapped. Their jobs depend on PR, they miss the student contact they used to have in the classroom so they like to see students, and any administering has a good bit of paperwork to go with it. Since even those who would like to can't do much to meet the ideal model, then what do we do with it?

I propose each school have a dean of faculty. He would be elected by the faculty, paid extra, given a reduced teaching load, and assigned the task of serving the faculty in whatever way he and the faculty see fit. Will you drink to that?

Coaches and Sports

In the high schools where I've taught, many teachers are also coaches. Coaches seem to have a few things in common. I've seen exceptions to these generalizations, but, admitting to a few exceptions, I believe them to be true.

Their enthusiasm for their sport is usually very high, almost a passion. They live it each hour they're awake. I like an enthusiastic attitude. I wish all teachers had the enthusiasm for their subjects that coaches have for their sports. Enthusiasm is contagious, students sense it and feel it, and I believe it to be a significant asset in approaching any task. Coaches usually have it and that's a very real plus. The more of it you have for whatever you teach, the better teacher you'll be.

While they're long on enthusiasm, I'm afraid they're short on scholarship. I generally find head coaches who teach academic subjects far more interested in their sport than in their subject area. They get by, they stay a few pages ahead of their students, and still I perceive them as coaches who also teach a certain subject and not as teachers who also coach. The closer to the top of the coaching staff, i.e., head coach of a major sport rather than assistant coach in a minor sport, the more apt their priorities are to be turned around: coaching first, teaching second.

I find the general emphasis on winning all out of proportion to its real educational value. Insofar as sports develop physical fitness, I'm all for them. Insofar as they teach the win-at-all-costs philosophy, I think they're corrupt. Not only do I find the emphasis on winning out of proportion, but the time they get is ridiculous.

Imagine an English teacher who went to his principal and proposed that two weeks before school started, the students were to show up twice a day, three hours at a time to practice their sentence structure. Once school started, they were to spend three hours each day after school on further practice. In addition, there were to be sessions on Saturday and sometimes on Sunday, and if a student misses any two of these sessions without a valid excuse, he's out of the class. In short, he wants twenty after-school hours a week and two full weeks before school starts for English practice. I can hear the principal now: "English is important, but let's not get carried away." If you've been around high school football practices, I think you get the message. Football can get what English cannot, and this is a sport that one of the major TV networks took a very careful look at and concluded it was just not safe. I know it may sound un-American to question such an institution, but I feel it gets too much time compared to academics, stresses winning disproportionately, and has a seriously questionable safety record.

My Three Favorite Books

Teaching and books must have something to do with one another. I hope teachers read books and encourage their students to do the same. Libraries are very nice places and full of all sorts of interesting information. It just so happens I have three favorite books that may provide some additional inspiration. I hope I'll soon read one that will push one of these three off the list. If you have three favorites, I'd like to know what they are and a little about them. I tell my students about my favorite books and I tell our librarian so he'll buy them. Please do the same.

The first one is *The Education of T.C. Mits* by Lillian R. Lieber. This is one of the very few truly readable math books I've ever seen. I'd trade all the math I learned in undergraduate school for what I learned reading this book, and the total reading time is two to four hours. I know it may sound too good to be true, but give it a try. You may consider this an unconditional rave review and she's written some others too, but I don't need to tell you about those 'cause once you read this one, you're a cinch to read them all.

Second on my list is *How to Make Money Owning Your Car (and Enjoy Every Minute of It)* by John R. Olson. It's described in Chapter 4, it's very good, and I wish I had written it myself.

Education and Ecstasy by George B. Leonard is the third. This is a book filled with hope. It was inspiring to read and made me proud to be a teacher, despite all the faults of the educational world.

9

Summary and Conclusions

The Summary

1. If teaching in America is a profession, it surely doesn't pay like one. While teaching is fun, you don't make much of a living, especially if you teach in a private school. The financial sacrifices imposed on teachers have been coped with in various ways, but there's very little chance to improve teaching pay and the situation grows worse while the financial future for teachers appears grim.

2. If you are willing to take some risks, and work with perseverance and passion, there's money to be made. Being a teacher may even be an advantage. Those same qualities it takes to be a good teacher are apt to make you good at business too.

3. To make money, get in business for yourself. Profits are the incentive, and there are tax advantages besides. Try to find a business where you'll have maximum control, flexible hours, minimum employees, one where you get more goods than good will for your investment, and one where the focus is on cash flow.

4. To acquire capital, you can moonlight but it's

147

tough, so learn while you earn. You may be able to
borrow on your life insurance or refinance your house.
Borrowing from banks must be carefully done. The
Small Business Administration can help. Friends and
relatives are a possible source of loans, and keeping
more of what you earn is easier than you might think
and will help give you the capital you need.

5. When actually starting a business, figure out the
finances, find the time, choose what you like from
what's available, locate close to home, and ask
questions about profits, time spent to operate, trends,
rates, and terms. Be certain you'll not only have a sound
investment but will be well paid for your time.
Franchising is a possibility. Treat failure as the price
of an education, and don't let those easy-to-think-of
excuses stop you. Get going. It doesn't take much
money and it's easier than teaching.

6. Don't spend a lot of money on frills but on tools,
and "tools" are a worthwhile expense. Keep prices well
ahead of costs and keep informed about your industry.
Critical purchasing can save lots of costs, and you can
purchase at some of the same discounts bigger
businesses do. Cultivate useful personal relationships
and choose partners with care. Then do your share of
the work and be willing to negotiate with your
partners. Spend your time as carefully as you do your
money. Set goals and make plans that lead to profits.

7. Besides making you a living while teaching full
time, your own successful business is apt to make you a

better teacher, more efficient, more confident, and comfortable. It may also tempt you to give up teaching or put a strain on family life. Keep a clear focus on why you're in business, and set careful priorities among family, teaching, and business.

8. Motivating students is tricky, so try to do it well and be satisfied with that. Keep the students strictly accountable for learning, and lead them to responsibility for their own learning while giving them opportunities to fail. Accountability in teaching is best demonstrated by the achievement-aptitude scores of the students, and student evaluation of teachers is an asset. Good teaching should be rewarded with money. Administrators of schools should be more concerned with service to the faculty. Coaches are apt to be models of enthusiasm, but their sports may get too much time and they tend to place disproportionate emphasis on winning.

Conclusions

"It's better to light one candle than to curse the darkness."

To become a teacher took patience, brains, willingness to learn, hard work, some inspiration, motivation, and determination. Now that you're on the other side of the desk, you have no doubt found it still takes all those things to do good work as a teacher. Fun it is, but easy it is not.

There's one more thing you may have found you need to stay in teaching: additional income. We can curse our pay and status and remain in teaching because we like it or think it is important. Or we can leave the field and probably find a better-paying job. But having a job you like is healthy for you, and liking teaching is very apt to help make you a fine teacher.

Those same things it takes to become a good teacher can be used to make you a success in business. You can do the two simultaneously and avoid having to make the financial sacrifices all too common to teachers. The dedication we need is to teaching and learning, not to financial sacrifice or strain. Put those same attributes to the simpler test. Making money *is* easier than teaching. I know.

I remember the first few days of teaching as a bit scary. The first attempt at your own business is a bit scary, too. Having done the former, you can do the latter; and once you've done the latter, I believe you'll be better at the former.

So, if you love teaching and want to stay and you don't care for financial strain, then I invite you to join me in the fun of TEACHING AND MAKING A LIVING AT THE SAME TIME.